Undergraduate Personality by Factored Scales

A large scale study on Cattell's 16PF and the Eysenck Personality Inventory

Peter Saville
Chief Psychologist NFER Test Department

Steve Blinkhorn
Lecturer in Psychology Hatfield Polytechnic

NFER Publishing Company Ltd.

Published by the NFER Publishing Company Ltd.,
2 Jennings Buildings, Thames Avenue,
Windsor, Berks. SL4 1QS
Registered Office: The Mere, Upton Park, Slough, Berks. SL1 2DQ
First Published 1976
© NFER Publishing Company Ltd., 1976
ISBN 0 85633 104 X

Printed in Great Britain by
Biddles of Guildford, Martyr Road, Guildford, Surrey.
Distributed in the USA by Humanities Press Inc.,
Hillary House—Fernhill House, Atlantic Highlands,
New Jersey, 07716, USA.

GENERAL NOTE

Associated Norm Tables (Saville and Blinkhorn, 1976) are published separately to the research described in this book and are available from the Test Department of the NFER Publishing Company.

British Undergraduate Norms to the 16PF (Forms A and B)

British Undergraduate Norms to the 16PF (Forms C and D)

British Undergraduate Norms to the IPAT Anxiety Scale,

Neuroticism Questionnaire and the Eysenck Personality Inventory (Form A)

Contents

PREFACE

This is is a book about evidence rather than about conclusions. We have set ourselves the task of providing, in a form which will prove convenient and comprehensible, the kind of information which a critical user of personality tests might reasonably expect to have available to facilitate the interpretation of test scores.

We have adopted a deliberately agnostic approach to the desirability of using these or any other personality questionnaires for practical purposes. We believe that the statistical analyses we present speak more clearly than any theoretical argument, and since we hope that this volume will become an indispensable aid to test users, we have taken care not to get involved in high-level debates about factoring methods and item characteristics. These considerations are, however, important and will be dealt with elsewhere.

Nonetheless, we are convinced that the results we present do have important implications and in striking a balance between the needs of the non-psychologist test user, the psychologist who uses these tests in research, and the test specialist, we hope we have not neglected unduly the needs of any group.

P F S
S F B

ACKNOWLEDGEMENTS

Our especial thanks are due to Mr Denis O'Donovan and Mr Tony Collin of the Nottingham University Careers Advisory Service for advice and help, particularly in the early stages of planning this project.

The work was carried out conjointly with the collection of validity data on the APU Occupational Interest Guide (Advanced version) and we gratefully acknowledge the cooperation of its author, Dr S.J. Closs of Edinburgh University, Department of Business Studies.

Facilities for the pilot study were provided at Glamorgan Polytechnic by Mr P. Hawkins, Head of the Department of Business Studies, with the cooperation of Mr N. Thomas, to both of whom we extend our thanks.

We would like to acknowledge the help of Mrs Janice Field, Mrs Iris Parry, Mrs Sheila Gray, Miss Laura Finlayson, Miss Irene Stevens and Mrs Julie Daly of the Test Department of the NFER Publishing Company.

Our appreciation is also extended to Mrs Jill Strong and her staff at the National Foundation for Educational Research. Extensive computing facilities were also made available at the Hatfield Polytechnic Computer Centre and particular thanks are due to Dr M.D. Sayers and Miss M. Clark for their cooperation.

We are in great debt to Mr Dan Simpson, Principal Lecturer in Computer Science at Sheffield Polytechnic, for all his help in certain analyses of the data.

We thank the Institute of Personality & Ability Testing (IPAT), the American publisher of the Cattell questionnaires, and the National Union of Students for their cooperation in the project. Our thanks are also due to Professor Dennis Child and Dr Paul Kline who provided helpful comments on drafts of the manuscript.

Chiefly, however, we must acknowledge the indispensible help of the 42 separate Careers and Appointments Services in the universities which took part. In undertaking to recruit the sample and arrange for the administration of the questionnaires they made this project possible. Whilst there is not space to name every individual concerned, we list below the organizations which provided us with our sample:

University of Aberdeen, Careers and Appointments Service,
University College of Wales, Aberystwyth, Careers and Appointments Service,
University of Aston in Birmingham, Appointments Office,
University College of North Wales, Bangor, Careers and Appointments Service,

The Queen's University of Belfast, Appointments and Careers Advisory Office,

University of Birmingham, Careers Service and Department of Psychology,

University of Bradford, Careers and Appointments Service,

University of Bristol, Careers Advisory Service,

University of Cambridge, Appointments Boards Career Advisory Service,

Cardiff Joint University Careers and Appointments Service,

The City University Appointments Service,

Dundee University, Careers and Appointments Service,

University of Durham, Careers Advisory Service,

University of East Anglia, Careers Centre,

University of Edinburgh, Careers and Appointments Advisory Service,

University of Essex, Careers Advisory Service,

University of Exeter, Appointments Board,

Heriot-Watt University, Careers Advisory Service,

University of Kent at Canterbury, Appointments Office,

Saint David's University College, Lampeter: the Academic Registrar,

University of Lancaster, Careers Advisory Service,

University of Leeds, Careers and Appointments Service,

University of Leicester, Careers and Appointments Service,

University College London, Careers Advisory Service,

University of London, Careers Advisory Service Central Office,

Loughborough University of Technology, Careers and Appointments Service,

University of Manchester, Careers and Appointments Service,

The New University of Ulster, Careers Advisory Service,

University of Newcastle-upon-Tyne, Careers Advisory Service,

University of Nottingham, Careers Advisory Service,

Oxford University, Appointments Committee,

University of Reading, Careers Advisory Service,

University of St Andrew's, Careers Advisory Service,

University of Salford, Careers and Appointments Service,

University of Sheffield, Careers Advisory Service,

University of Stirling, Careers Advisory Service,

University of Strathclyde, Student Advisory Service,

University of Sussex, Appointments Advisory Service,

University College of Swansea, Careers Advisory Service,

University of Warwick, Careers Advisory Service,

University of York, Careers Service.

Finally, we give our sincere thanks to all those students who volunteered their time by cooperating in the project.

LIST OF TABLES

Chapter 4

LIST OF FIGURES

Chapter 1

Introduction

The personality questionnaire

It is generally believed that Francis Galton devised the first questionnaires in the 1880s for his studies of mental imagery at his Kensington laboratory. His statement in the *Fortnightly Review* of 1884 that 'the character which shapes our conduct is a definite and durable "something" and therefore . . . . it is reasonable to attempt *t* measure it' is not unlike many contemporary views of personality.

Despite the problems associated with the questionnaire approach to personality measurement — one is reminded of the comment of Sir Frederic Bartlett reported by Buzzard (1971), 'I don't know . . . they may be all right . . . they always seem to me to overestimate the self-knowledge of the subject and to underestimate his sense of humour' — the technique flourished after World War I, until, in the 1970s there are literally hundreds of published instruments.

Most self-report personality questionnaires consist of a series of statements or questions about the individual, his interests and attitudes. These the subject endorses according to his strength of agreement. To make scoring easier and more dependable, the subject is usually required to select the most appropriate answer from choices provided in the questionnaire form. The choices in the items which make up an inventory are usually presented in one of three ways.

First there is the true / false technique of, for example, the Eysenck Personality Inventory, where the subject has to choose between two clear-cut alternatives.

I enjoy going to parties.
a.   b.
Yes   No

This approach has the advantage of being statistically manageable (*cf* the pass / fail dichotomy on an ability test item) and helps to overcome certain types of bias. However, it can become frustrating to the respondent who may find it both difficult and unnatural to answer every item on a yes / no basis. There is the danger that the item format will cause the subject to challenge the sense of questions being asked him, and so become inconsistent in his answers. Indeed, it is not unknown for respondents to invent a middle response category!

A second approach is the use of the 'forced choice' technique, where one or more of a number of alternatives are chosen by the subject as most or least characteristic of himself. For example:

Mark the statement which shows which you prefer doing:
a.   Going to parties.
b.   Reading a serious book.

Inventories based on this system are the Gordon Personal Profile, the Gordon Personal Inventory and the Edwards Personal Preference Schedule (EPPS). One attraction of this approach is that by matching the items, social desirability response sets (the tendency for subjects to put up a good front and show socially acceptable characteristics) can to some extent be controlled. In practice it has proved difficult to match items exactly in terms of social desirability and it appears that instruments like the EPPS can in fact be deliberately faked to create more favourable impressions (Dicken, 1959). It is probable also that items matched in social desirability for one occupation or set of circumstances will not be matched for other occupations or other sets of circumstances. In addition because certain personality types are more prone to presenting answers in a favourable light, it has been argued that attempting to eradicate the effects of social desirability is like throwing the baby out with the bath water.

Another problem concerns scaling properties. The strength of each variable is gauged relative to the strengths of all other variables and as a result it is impossible to gain high or low scores across all scales. Cattell (1944) has termed this 'ipsative' measurement and strictly we should not compare scores of different individuals although this is often done and extensive norm tables produced. (For more information on this point see Anastasi, 1961, and Cattell, 1944.)

The third type of item format is an extension from the true / false item to three or more possible choices. For example:

I like going to parties
a.   b.   c.
True   False   ?

or

> I like going to parties
> a.   b.   c.
> Frequently   Occasionally   Never

or

I like going to parties
a.   b.   c.   d.   e.
Always   Frequently   Occasionally   Rarely   Never

The first example is similar to the method of item presentation in the Minnesota Multiphasic Personality Inventory (MMPI) and the second to the personality questionnaires developed by R.B. Cattell. This approach is more acceptable to the subject although the dimensionality of the middle response is often a problem, especially if it becomes a waste-bin category of 'don't knows', 'in betweens', 'occasionally's' and 'I don't understand the question'. In these multiple choice formats the effects of faking and social desirability are not so much controlled but detected by lie, motivational distortion and other such keys. In the case where there are three choices the responses become statistically less manageable whilst five or more may cause a practical problem in the hand marking of the questionnaires.

Obviously with most questionnaire items the prior assumption has already been made that the underlying trait represents a continuum. It is not usually acceptable for a subject to endorse two answers even though he may feel that both are equally appropriate and it is this lack of flexibility which many criticize in the questionnaire approach.

Goldberg (1970), commenting upon the current proliferation of personality inventories ('inventory' and 'questionnaire' will be used interchangeably throughout this report), distinguished between those inventories developed in response to pressures from society to deal with specific problems and those stemming from theoretical concepts about the nature of personality. In the first group are questionnaires like the California Psychological Inventory (CPI), designed to measure practical outcomes of social behaviour, and the Minnesota Multiphasic Personality Inventory (MMPI), which measures aspects of personal adjustment, and those which are concerned with vocational choice, such as the Strong Vocational Interest Blank. Instruments of this kind tend to be constructed on an empirical basis where items are selected which discriminate between different groups of people.

The second category of questionnaire includes the inventory

measures of introversion—extraversion, those based on Murray's (1938) system of needs like the Edwards Personal Preference Schedule, those which are psychoanalytic in conception like the Dynamic Personality Inventory and the group of questionnaires which make up what has been termed the factor analytic school.

The factor analytic approach to personality measurement.

Many questionnaires have been produced, each, as Cronbach (1970) has pointed out, using items from its predecessors, adding new ones and scoring them in new combinations of traits and scales. Cattell (1973) has written ' . . . let us be clear that nothing stops anyone from making up questionnaires for any trait he cares to imagine and since there are an indefinitely large number of conceivable traits and roughly 50,000 psychologists, questionnaires have in fact been the prolific rabbits of the psychomobic world!'

Trait names become a source of much confusion. What was 'Introversion' to one author was not introversion to another; 'Dominance' in system X bore a striking resemblance to the trait of aggression in system Y. It was the construction of what appeared to be arbitrary personality scales that the factor analysts attacked. The only way to resolve this Tower of Babel, the factor analytic school argued, was to 'discover' clearly defined personality variables, building blocks, which would serve the psychologist as the table of elements serves the chemist. Rather than have a multitude of scales to predict all sorts of social, educational and clinical outcomes (the criterion — related or empirical approach) is it not possible to find a basic set of constructs by which we can understand human personality? The factor analysts believe it is.

Although there is considerable variation within the school the basic principles are simple. Working with a set of questionnaire scales which has been administered to a large group of subjects, it is possible to measure the degree of association between the variables by correlating every scale with every other scale. The correlations between each pair of variables are represented in a correlation matrix as in the example, Table 1.1.

It will be noticed that the columns (read down) below the main diagonal of the matrix contain the same values as the rows (read across) above the diagonal. Looking closely at Table 1.1, we can ask whether any of these hypothetical variables are related to any degree with one another. For example, do subjects consistently gain a high score on one scale and not on another? The latter is clearly the case with scales R and S; the negative correlation of −0.92 means that there is a strong tendency for those getting high scores on Scale R to get low scores on

Table 1.1. Example of a hypothetical 5x5 correlation matrix

		Variable			
		R	S	T	X	Y
Variable	R		−.92	.13	−.11	.82
	S	−.92		.01	.27	−.86
	T	.13	.01		.89	.08
	X	−.11	.27	.89		.21
	Y	.82	−.86	.08	.21	

Scale S and vice versa. The direction of the relationship is of no major importance because it merely reflects the scoring conventions of the scales, but what is important is the presence of a strong association between the two variables. Indeed the relationship is so high that we might wonder whether these scales were in any way distinct and whether R and S are simply different names for the same underlying variable.

Visual inspection of this correlation matrix suggests the presence of two underlying dimensions or 'factors' — the first common to variables R,S and Y and the second to T and X. The factor analysis of correlation coefficients is a decision making process which goes beyond simple visual inspection to estimate the strength of each influence — our example illustrates the logic of factor analysis but lacks its refinements. It is not possible for us to go into a detailed explanation of the principles of factor analysis here but good introductions have been provided by Child (1970) and Gorsuch (1974). Factor analysis has been used in scale construction and as part of a complex theory of personality by three main psychologists: J.P. Guilford and R.B. Cattell in the United States and H.J. Eysenck in Britain.

The Guilford-Zimmerman Temperament Survey (1949–1955) was one of the early personality inventories to be developed through the techniques of factor analysis. The questionnaire gave scores on the following ten factors, each score based on thirty items: General Activity, Restraint, Ascendance, Sociability, Emotional Stability, Objectivity, Friendliness, Thoughtfulness, Personal Relations and Masculinity. However, the Guilford-Zimmerman Temperament Survey is not commonly used in Britain and was not included in this study.

The Cattell Personality Questionnaires

Cattell (1950) has provided us with a deliberately general definition of personality as 'that which permits a prediction of what a person will do in a given situation. The goal of psychological research in personality is thus to establish laws about what different people will do in all kinds of social and general environmental situations . . . personality is . . . . concerned with *all* the behaviour of the individual, both overt and under the skin.'

As we have already noted, the Sixteen Personality Factor Questionnaire (16PF), developed by Cattell and his associates in the United States, has found wide acceptance in Britain, Ireland and the rest of the Western World. Buros (1972) shows a yearly average of 80 references between 1965 and 1969 for the 16PF and the trend is upwards.

The instrument has been put to a multitude of uses, impossible to review here but the list includes studies on academic achievement (Warburton *et al*., 1963; Cortis, 1968), teacher training (Start, 1966, 1968), computer programmers (Morris and Martin, 1972), birth order (Allman and White, 1968), racing drivers (Johnsgard and Ogilvie, 1968), sensory deprivation (Arnhoff and Lean, 1963), angina pectoris (Bakker and Levenson, 1967) and hypnotic susceptibility (Hartman, 1966).

Cattell has never held that the sole or even the best method of investigating human personality is the questionnaire. Whilst it is true, possibly as a result of the practical advantages and economies of the self-report technique, that his work has in recent years centred on the questionnaire, Cattell has strongly emphasized the importance of ratings and laboratory tests in personality measurement.

It was in fact by way of observer ratings (termed 'Life-data'), that Cattell's major dimensions of personality were derived (Cattell, 1943). Using the adjectives and adverbs descriptive of behaviour listed in the English dictionary, Cattell first defined the clusters upon which his traits were to be based by eliminating synonyms and visually inspecting correlation matrices and not as is commonly supposed by factor analysis: neither factor analysis nor computer technology were then sufficiently advanced to allow the large scale analyses which Cattell and others have worked on since the late 1950s.

Cattell regards the life record (L-data) self-rating (Q-data) and objective test (T-data) as different ways of measuring the fundamental traits which are descriptive of human personality. Much time has been spent, not always with complete success (Becker, 1960), in attempting to match the factors across these three approaches to personality measurement. To Cattell and his associates it is rather like a man using a ruler and a chain to measure the area of a field. There will be variations in that the units of measurement may differ, but essentially the same picture will evolve.

It is perhaps a little surprising that Cattell should have so early adopted this view. After all it is not unreasonable to suspect that the constructs used by an individual in rating himself may vary from those used to rate others. Such difficulties have been acknowledged in practice by the presence, for example, of four factors in the 16PF which have not been discovered in L or T data.

At the first level of Cattell's model of personality, there are the many surface traits of personality. Surface traits are the directly observable aspects of human behaviour, the labels which are frequently used in our everyday experience. It is the first order factors or primary source traits which the 16PF seeks to measure and which are claimed to represent the universal basic variables in the total personality structure. They are defined both by letters of the alphabet and technical names coined by Cattell. Popularly descriptive labels are also provided for a more ready understanding of their nature. Missing source traits are often to be found in other questionnaires, for example Factor D (Excitability), appears in the High School Personality Questionnaire for 12- to 16-year-olds, but is not included in the adult 16PF.

Cattell's main first order factors as measured by the 16PF are listed in Table 1.2. Although 16 factors are described, Cattell has suggested in more recent work (1973) that upwards of 25 may eventually be required to describe human personality.

The order of primaries in the 16PF is based on their decreasing contribution to behavioural variance as estimated from Cattell's studies. It is important to note that whilst Cattell refers to the first orders as functionally unitary, they are oblique factors. This means that some correlation exists between them; for example people who are forthright (N−) tend to be assertive and competitive (E+).

Because of these correlations between the primary source traits it has been possible to factor analyse these scales to some eight second order factors, (Table 1.3). Again, both technical and popular names are utilized to describe these secondaries. Cattell has always been insistent that although these second orders can be broadly descriptive, they cannot be used without losing a certain degree of information and precision. Cattell has also advocated the existence of third and fourth orders but these are little researched at the present time.

The first editions of the 16PF appeared in the early 1950s with the issue of revisions over the next 15 years or so. The latest and most refined versions were published in 1968 and 1969 — parallel (alternate) Forms A and B, each of 187 items and the somewhat easier language Forms C and D each of 105 items. Forms A and B take approximately 50 minutes each to complete and C and D approximately 35 minutes. In addition to the main primaries and secondaries, Cattell has provided weights to apply to the first order scales for the calculation of four 'derived criteria'. These are amorphous measures related to external

Table 1.2: First order (primary) factors of the 16PF

Low Score Description	Source Trait	High Score Description
Reserved, detached, critical, aloof (*Sizothymia*)	A	Outgoing, warmhearted, easy-going, participating (*Affectothymia, formerly cyclothymia*)
Less intelligent, concrete-thinking (*Lower scholastic mental capacity*)	B	More intelligent, abstract-thinking, bright (*Higher scholastic mental capacity*)
Affected by feelings, emotionally less stable, easily upset (*Lower ego strength*)	C	Emotionally stable, faces reality, calm, mature (*Higher ego strength*)
Humble, mild, accommodating, conforming (*Submissiveness*)	E	Assertive, aggressive, stubborn, competitive (*Dominance*)
Sober, prudent, serious, taciturn (*Desurgency*)	F	Happy-go-lucky, impulsively lively, gay, enthusiastic (*Surgency*)
Expedient, disregards rules, feels few obligations (*Weaker superego strength*)	G	Conscientious, persevering, staid, moralistic (*Stronger superego strength*)
Shy, restrained, timid, threat-sensitive (*Threctia*)	H	Venturesome, socially bold, uninhibited, spontaneous (*Parmia*)
Tough-minded, self-reliant, realistic, no-nonsense (*Harria*)	I	Tender-minded, clinging, over-protected, sensitive (*Premsia*)
Trusting, adaptable, free of jealousy, easy to get along with (*Alaxia*)	L	Suspicious, self-opinionated, hard to fool (*Protension*)
Practical, careful, conventional, regulated by external realities, proper (*Praxernia*)	M	Imaginative, wrapped up in inner urgencies, careless of practical matters, bohemian (*Autia*)
Forthright, natural, artless, unpretentious (*Artlessness*)	N	Shrewd, calculating, worldly, penetrating (*Shrewdness*)
Self-assured, confident, serene (*Untroubled adequacy*)	O	Apprehensive, self-reproaching, worrying, troubled (*Guilt proneness*)
Conservative, respecting established ideas, tolerant of traditional difficulties (*Conservatism*)	Q1	Experimenting, liberal, analytical, free-thinking (*Radicalism*)
Group-dependent, A 'joiner' and sound follower (*Group adherence*)	Q2	Self-sufficient, prefers own decisions, resourceful (*Self-sufficiency*)
Undisciplined self-conflict, follows own urges, careless of protocol (*Low integration*)	Q3	Controlled, socially precise, following self-image (*High self-concept control*)
Relaxed, tranquil, unfrustrated (*Low ergic tension*)	Q4	Tense, frustrated, driven, overwrought (*High ergic tension*)

Table 1.3: Second order factors of the 16PF

Low Score Description	Second Order Factors	High Score Description	Chief First Order Factors Involved
INTROVERSION Invia	QI	EXTRAVERSION Exvia	A+, E+, F+, H+, Q2−
LOW ANXIETY Adjustment	QII	HIGH ANXIETY Anxiety	C−, H−, L+, O+, Q3−, Q4+
SENSITIVITY Pathemia	QIII	TOUGH POISE Cortertia	A−, I−, M−, E+, L+
DEPENDENCE Subduedness	QIV	INDEPENDENCE Independence	E+, L+, M+, Q1+, Q2+
NATURALNESS	QV	DISCREETNESS	N+, A+, M−, O−
COOL REALIST	QVI	PRODIGAL SUBJECTIVITY	I+, M+, L−
LOW INTELLIGENCE	QVII	HIGH INTELLIGENCE	B+
LOW SUPEREGO STRENGTH	QVIII	HIGH SUPEREGO STRENGTH	G+, Q3+, F−

criteria which he has named Neuroticism, Leadership, School Achievement and Creativity. It should also be noted that because Forms C and D of the 16PF are more often used in occupational selection they contain a Motivational Distortion (MD) Scale. The MD scale is an experimental variable made up of items which show maximum shift from an anonymous to a job seeking situation and correlate most with shifts in the personality factors in the same situational change.

Two further questionnaires are outgrowths of Cattell's system. The IPAT Anxiety Scale (1963), otherwise known as the Self Analysis Form, was designed as a brief, easily administered means of measuring Cattell's second order factor QII, Anxiety. It consists of items loading the five factors which principally contribute to the second order Anxiety factor: the weighting of these five is achieved by varying the number of items in proportion to the weight each factor should bear. The factors are: C (negatively loaded), L,O,Q3,Q4. (see Table 1.3.)

Anxiety is clearly a factor of considerable clinical interest and Cattell has devoted much energy to distinguishing it from Neuroticism, which, he claims, is not a pure factor but a syndrome of which anxiety is a part. The Neuroticism Scale Questionnaire (1961) was designed as a measure of this syndrome, or to use Cattell's term, 'derived criterion'. Similar in construction to the IPAT Anxiety Scale, it has items loading Factors I,F and E as well as the second order Anxiety factor.

Finally, although they will not form any part of this research, we should mention the questionnaires which Cattell has developed for measuring children's personality (High School Personality Questionnaire, Children's Personality Questionnaire and Early School Personality Questionnaire), motivation — (Motivation Analysis Test and School Motivation Analysis Test) and pathological dimensions (Clinical Analysis Questionnaire).

The Eysenck Personality Inventory

If Eysenck has been less prolific than Cattell in constructing questionnaires, this has not been the case when it has come to expounding his theories of personality. Eysenck views personality as the stable and enduring organization of a person's character, temperament, intellect and physique. For Eysenck (1947) personality is the ' . . . sum-total of the actual or potential behaviour-patterns of the organism, as determined by heredity and environment: it originates and develops through the functional interaction of the four main sectors into which these behaviour — patterns are organized; the cognitive sector (intelligence), the conative sector (character), the affective sector (temperament), and the somatic sector (constitution).'

Like Cattell, Eysenck is more interested in comparing characteristics of an individual with the characteristics of people in general than with how characteristics are related within the individual — what have been termed respectively the nomothetic and idiographic approaches to the study of personality.

Eysenck uses the concepts of trait and type in his work. Traits are made up from the habitual responses of the individual and represent a consistency for certain types of behaviour across different situations. The personality type refers to a group of traits which tend to be correlated or clustered together; it is the highest level of organization in the personality.

From factor analysis based on large numbers of cases Eysenck has proposed the two major personality dimensions of Extraversion and Neuroticism (see Figure 1.1), with two other independent factors of psychotism and intelligence.

The Eysenck Personality Inventory (EPI) was constructed to tap these dimensions and with the 16PF is without doubt the most commonly used measure of adult personality in these islands. The EPI (1964), a development of the Maudsley Personality Inventory, consists of the two parallel forms A and B, each made up of 57 forced-choice items, and contains a lie scale which may be used to detect subjects

---

Figure 1.1: Eysenck's Two Factor Model of Personality (From Eysenck and Eysenck, 1964)

Relationship of Extraversion/Introversion and Neuroticism/Stability to earlier personality schemes

showing a desirability response set.

Whilst Eysenck and Cattell are in broad agreement that personality is best described in terms of factored scales, their methods are different and their rivalry well-known. Whilst Cattell looks for oblique primary factors whose intercorrelations will yield higher order factors, Eysenck prefers orthogonal factors with, in consequence, no possibility of factoring to a higher order. Cattell thus accuses Eysenck of underfactoring (i.e. producing too few factors), whilst Eysenck levels the contrary charge at Cattell, claiming in addition that Cattell's primary factors are unreliable. There is a good deal of evidence, however, that Eysenck's two factors, Extraversion and Neuroticism, match rather closely the first two of Cattell's second order factors, Exvia and Anxiety.

Aims of the study

With the possible exception of the Norway rat, social scientists have studied no animal more thoroughly than the university undergraduate. As a constant and easily accessible source of volunteer subjects for experiment, the student body has made a considerable contribution to the scientific advances of psychology.

There remain, however, questions which cannot be answered by laboratory experiment. How representative of mankind is the undergraduate? How does he compare with other young people outside the universities, or with his counterparts in other countries? Are there differences between male and female undergraduates and are these differences the same as those between other men and women and between students of other lands? These questions can only be answered by field research of the kind that is reported in this study.

Accessibility to the experimenter is not the only characteristic which distinguishes the university undergraduate. To borrow Wiseman's (1973) phrase, 'he or she is one of the winners of the "educational obstacle race." Course failure, for any reason and of any kind, will not only prove costly but may mean that entrance to many professions is blocked. *It is an important aim of this study therefore that it should investigate how factored personality questionnaires can help us understand the university undergraduate.*

The second aim of the study is a matter of technology rather than pure research. Until recently the lack of British normative data on the Sixteen Personality Factor Questionnaire (16PF), developed by R.B. Cattell in the United States, handicapped the researcher and applied user alike. It was to remedy this deficiency that the British Adult Standardization of Forms A and B of the 16PF was undertaken

(Saville, 1972). Nevertheless, it is the university student, whether at the point of embarking on a career, or in dealings with student counselling services or as a volunteer subject in research, who is perhaps most likely to encounter the questionnaire. *Hence, the project described in this book was set up with the second aim of producing normative data suitable for application to university undergraduates and young graduates and by extension to those following degree courses in colleges and polytechnics.*

We do not subscribe to the view that the trait labels used here are the only valid ways of describing personality, nor for that matter that the questionnaire is necessarily the best method of investigating personality. What we do recognize is a need for more technical information when in Britain and Ireland somewhere in the region of a quarter of a million testing sessions, using the questionnaires developed by Cattell and Eysenck, are conducted annually.

Whilst much of this usage is for research purposes in the universities, there has been a noticeable trend in Britain over the past ten years or so to apply these questionnaires clinically and in job selection and placement. This practice has grown to the extent that the British Psychological Society, unlike any other professional body of psychologists in the world, has directly sanctioned the use of personality tests in staff selection, by approving courses for non-psychologists in the use and interpretation of Cattell's Sixteen Personality Factor Questionnaire. As most professional bodies are usually willing to release only the most well-tried of techniques into the hands of non-professionals, the clear implication is that such inventories can be potentially valuable instruments in predicting the complex of behaviour which we term 'job performance.' Considering the challenge that academic psychology has lacked applicability in everyday life, this is an achievement indeed! *Because of this usage and because uncommitted British evaluations have been few, an examination of the psychometric properties of these scales is our third main aim.*

The work of H.J. Eysenck in Britain and R.B. Cattell in the USA is well known. Together they form what has been termed the 'establishment' in factor analytic personality research. Despite the hard-headed approach of these, the main protagonists of factor analysis in questionnaire construction, personality measurement is an emotive topic and it is certainly all too easy to become involved in controversy. There are many who would act as judge and executioner without having heard the evidence; there are others who hold an almost mystical reverence for measurement by questionnaire. There are difficulties also in remaining apart from the various schools of thought when undertaking research in this area. *Nevertheless, it is our fourth aim that this book will facilitate a clearer appraisal of the work of Eysenck and Cattell.*

Thus, this is a study both in education and in psychological measurement. It is research in education because we shall be using factored personality scales to describe undergraduate personality. It is research in psychological measurement because the data obtained from our student sample will be used to investigate the psychometric properties of the scales in question.

Whilst this report is principally intended for users of the instruments, for researchers, for the University Appointments Boards and for those who are already acquainted with the rudiments of personality measurement by factored scales, we hope that we have provided sufficient background information for this book to be of interest to the less specialized reader also. Our main concern will be with scale characteristics and it is not our intention to become heavily involved at this stage in factor analysis, itemetrics or controversy over the 'true structure of personality'. Perhaps we should make an apology regarding the many pages of data which we report, most of which are contained in Chapter 3. We have come to appreciate fully Robert Louis Stevenson's observation that art is the knowledge of what to leave out, but it was very clear from requests which we received during the compilation of this book that as full a breakdown of the results as possible would be desirable. Hence, although we have provided summary text and observations, this report is inevitably about data.

Design of the Study

The questionnaires

Forms A, B, C and D of the Sixteen Personality Factor Questionnaire (16PF), the IPAT Anxiety Scale (IAS), the Neuroticism Scale Questionnaire (NSQ) and Form A of the Eysenck Personality Inventory (EPI) were used in the study. In the case of the 16PF the 1968 Edition of Forms A and B and the 1969 Edition of Forms C and D, have been used in this research and standardization. These are psychometrically more advanced than earlier editions and, as Cattell has pointed out, much of the criticism of the 16PF structure made by Eysenck (1969), Levonian (1961) and others has become obsolete with their publication. British editions of the 16PF, which contain minor amendments of item content in terms of anglicized grammar and expression (e.g. color to colour) were preferred to the original American versions.

The fieldwork

The fieldwork was organized with respect to two main studies. In the first, Forms A and B of the 16PF were administered (this we shall refer to as the A / B study). In the second, Forms C and D of the 16PF the IPAT Anxiety Scale (IAS) and the Neuroticism Scale Questionnaire (NSQ), together with Form A of the EPI were used (this we shall call the C / D study). That is, each student completed either the 16PF Forms A and B or the 16PF Forms C and D plus the IAS, NSQ and EPI. The order of administration of forms of the 16PF was counterbalanced in the two studies in order to eliminate differential administration order effects, half of each sample completing Form A (or C) first, the other half completing Form B (or D) first. This was achieved by manipulation of the page orders in the printed booklets before stitching. The administration orders are schematized in Table 2.1.

Table 2.1— British undergraduate standardisation administration order (N = 2584)

A/B Study		C/D Study	
Group 1	Group 2	Group 3	Group 4
		IAS	IAS
		+	+
16PF Form A	16PF Form B	16PF Form C	16PF Form D
+	+	+	+
16PF Form B	16PF Form A	16PF Form D	16PF Form C
		+	+
		NSQ	NSQ
		+	+
		EPI Form A	EPI Form A
Female = 339	Female = 339	Female = 344	Female = 344
N Male = 309	N Male = 304	N Male = 305	N Male = 300
Total = 648	Total = 643	Total = 649	Total = 644

In the printed booklets, the original type of the Cattell inventories was reproduced lithographically, whereas the EPI had to be reset. The students marked their answers directly in the booklets by ringing the appropriate answer in the 16PF, or placing an 'X' in the appropriate box in the other questionnaires. This method of response has the advantage of eliminating the transcription errors which may occur when a separate answer sheet is used and was adopted in the general population standardization of the 16PF (Saville, 1972). It also reduces administration time.

Questionnaire administration

Two basic administration methods were adopted: group sessions and individual administration. The universities were given the option of which method to adopt: many used both. In most of the participating universities administration was carried out by University Appointments Officers who were psychologists or who had been trained in psychological measurement. The authors undertook administration at some of the London colleges and at Brunel University. At Birmingham University, the Department of Psychology undertook administration on behalf of the Careers Service.

Students were given a good deal of background information to the study and the instructions on the printed booklet were supplemented by serveral pages of instructions to the field workers. No problems of any moment arose in the course of administration.

Participants followed the standard administration instructions to the various questionnaires and were encouraged to work as quickly as possible: 90 minutes was suggested as the average time needed to complete the questionnaires, and this, in general, proved to be a realistic estimate.

The fieldwork was carried out between March and June of 1973. Completed booklets were returned by the universities to the Test Department of the NFER Publishing Company where they were coded and checked for errors. At this stage some two dozen booklets were removed from the study, mainly for reasons of incomplete data. The edited scripts were punched on to cards and the scoring of the questionnaires carried out by computer.

The sample

All the University Appointments Services in the United Kingdom were invited to take part in the fieldwork: three refused, one did not reply and adverse circumstances prevented three others from actually producing a sample. Every other university took part and is represented in the final sample, making a total of 43 universities and university colleges, counting Oxford, Cambridge and London as one each, and the colleges of the University of Wales as separate institutions.

The sample consists of undergraduates in their second year at university (not necessarily their penultimate year) in the academic year 1972–73. This choice was deliberate. First year undergraduates are new to the university environment and have experienced a total disruption of their social, family and academic lives. The final year student is not always easily accessible and is under the considerable pressures of final examinations. In short, undergraduates in their second year are acclimatized to the university environment without being unduly pressurized by the threat of examination and so were chosen as the most appropriate group on which to base this study.

The sample was selected by a variety of random and quasi-random methods by the fieldworkers: in all cases each participant was approached individually whether by letter or by personal contact. Ultimately a total sample of 2584 was obtained approximately equally split by sex and across the two standardization groups.

The overall response rate was approximately 50 per cent: in some centres it was of course lower than this whilst others managed rates as high as 90 per cent depending greatly upon the resources available to the university at the time of the project. The cost for example of physically tracking down every member of a randomly drawn sample (this was in fact done in a few universities) would have been prohibitive, so the most common approach was to invite the selected students to attend any one of a number of group testing sessions.

Table 2.2: Characteristics of the standardization sample 16PF Forms A / B Study

	Females (N = 678)		Males (N = 613)		Total Sexes (N = 1291)	
	University Population %	*Standardization Sample* %	*University Population* %	*Standardization Sample* %	*University Population* %	*Standardization Sample* %
University Region						
Wales	7	9	6	8	6	8
West England	6	6	5	5	5	6
South East England	12	9	14	10	13	10
London*	12	11	12	9	13	10
East Anglia	4	5	7	9	6	7
Midlands	12	11	11	11	11	11
Northern England	26	28	26	25	26	26
Scotland	17	15	15	17	16	16
Northern Ireland	4	6	4	6	4	6
University Type And Size						
Large Provincial	37	34	32	30	33	32
Medium Provincial	29	31	29	32	29	31
Small Provincial	18	22	18	21	18	21
London University	12	8	11	8	12	8
Oxbridge	4	6	10	9	8	8
Subject Area						
Arts, Professional, Vocational	40	35	17	17	25	27
Science, Agriculture, Engineering	25	29	52	54	43	41
Social Sciences	25	31	22	25	23	27
Medicine, Dentistry Health	10	6	9	4	9	5

* Including the City University

Table 2.3: Characteristics of the standardization sample

16PF Forms C / D Study

	Females (N = 688) %		Male (N = 605) %		Total Sexes (N = 1293) %	
	University Population	Standardization Sample	University Population	Standardization Sample	University Population	Standardization Sample
University Region						
Wales	7	9	6	9	6	9
West England	6	4	5	4	5	4
South East England	12	8	14	9	13	9
London*	12	10	12	7	13	9
East Anglia	4	5	7	9	6	7
Midlands	12	12	11	13	11	12
Northern England	26	27	26	26	26	26
Scotland	17	17	15	17	16	16
Northern Ireland	4	7	4	6	4	6
University Type and Size						
Large Provincial	37	34	32	33	33	33
Medium Provincial	29	31	29	31	29	31
Small Provincial	18	20	18	21	18	20
London University	12	9	11	6	12	7
Oxbridge	4	6	10	9	8	8
Subject Area						
Arts, Professional, Vocational	40	34	17	15	25	25
Science, Agriculture, Engineering	25	30	52	52	43	41
Social Sciences	25	30	22	28	23	29
Medicine, Dentistry Health	10	6	9	5	9	5

* Including the City University.

Tables 2.2 and 2.3 give the percentages of respondents in the standardization sample compared with the percentages of undergraduate entrants in the year in which the sample entered university.

University type and size is a hybrid classification: Oxford and Cambridge, the University of London and the University of Wales were first allocated to separate categories. The remainder of the universities were classified according to the number of undergraduates entering 1970–71. 'Small' is defined as having fewer than 800 undergraduate entrants in 1970–71. Similarly 'Medium' means an undergraduate entry of 800–1500 and 'large' 1500 or more in the same year.

University region is determined according to the map on page 35. Subject area is a reduction of the University Grants Committee's ninefold classification of degree subjects into four categories. Arts and professional and vocational subjects correspond to UGC categories 7, 8 and 9; science, agriculture and engineering to UGC 3, 4 and 5; social sciences to 1 and 6; medicine etc., is UGC category 2.

It is difficult to assess the extent to which our sample may justifiably be claimed to be representative of the undergraduate population as a whole. Certainly it is far more representative than a group obtained from just one or two universities, and the restriction to second-year undergraduates circumvented the problems associated with obtaining a sample which is homogeneous across the universities. That is to say, we do not have the problem of combining a large group of freshmen from one university with a clutch of postgraduates from another. Moreover the standardization group was tested under clearly defined conditions between March and June 1973. It is not a hodge-podge of data collected from many different sources and answer sheets completed under largely unknown circumstances.

The problem of volunteer samples is of course one which besets all research in the social sciences. Nevertheless, there is circumstantial evidence that the sample is not unduly biased in this respect. We shall see in later sections, for example, that variance on the personality scales is not restricted in comparison with general population adults where the response rate was somewhat higher (Saville, 1972): that results on the EPI do not differ significantly from Eysenck's (1964) main student standardization sample and that, as far as we can tell, the distribution of degree class in the sample is close to that in the student population as a whole.

Furthermore, the demographic characteristics suggest that we have obtained a relatively good representative sample of the undergraduate population. Perhaps the most noticeable discrepancy between the sample and the university population is in the case of male students following courses in medicine, dentistry and health (nine per cent in the university population as against four per cent in the standardization

Figure 2.1: British undergraduate standardization of the 16PF geographical distribution of the participants' universities

sample). In all other respects the sample and population percentages show a reasonably close match. However, it should be borne in mind that our sample was essentially a volunteer sample. It was based on quota rather than random sampling; universities were asked to fill quotas with respect to their size and region. No payment was made for participation; in approaching the prospective participants, altruistic motives were stressed — the future value of having good British norms available to ensure maximum possible accuracy and utility of what are, after all, commonly used measures.

Apart from the dubious ethics of pressurizing individuals unduly to obtain increased response rates, there is the danger of distortion and sabotage of response. We shall observe that the mean score of this sample on the EPI Lie Scale is of about the same order as that reported by Eysenck (1964) and, in fact, considerably lower on the 16PF Motivational Distortion Scale than corresponding figures provided by Cattell in his norm supplements. These findings support the view that the questionnaires were completed in an appropriate motivational state.

The authors believe that the sample is about as representative a group of the undergraduate population as can be obtained without recourse to regiments of interviewers cornering a perfectly selected random sample in their college rooms and forcing them to participate at gunpoint — a technique which in any case might lead to undesirable motivational and attitudinal distortion, casting in doubt the value of the data for normative purposes.

It is, however, important to remember that anonymity and confidentiality were guaranteed, hence our sample had no reason to try to present itself in a particularly favourable light. The experienced test user will be aware of the implications of this fact when using these data for occupational selection purposes.

Chapter 3

Group Differences

The questionnaires used in this project, like all psychometric devices, are principally designed to describe, in terms of scales which have some claim to scientific objectivity, differences between individuals. There is, therefore, an underlying assumption that there are real differences between individuals in their behaviour which may, to some extent at least, be measured. Indeed, the scales in the 16PF are listed in order of the amount of variability in behaviour that they describe. We therefore expected that groups which, on a commonsense basis, might appear to be different in terms of personality, would show different patterns of scores on the various questionnaires.

Two methods are available for the study of group differences. Most straightforwardly one may test for the significance of differences between mean scores on each scale for each group: this approach has been used many times before and by adopting it here we are merely following a well-trodden path.

However, when the scales concerned are related, that is to say when non-zero correlations are found between the scales, as is the case with the 16PF, such a method may result in the exaggeration of underlying differences. For instance, as we shall see, the difference between the sexes on Factor O in our sample is of about the same order as the difference on Factor Q4. Yet the correlation between these two scales tends to be high: it may therefore be that the difference found is simply reflected in both scores because of their correlation.

Nonetheless, we feel justified in presenting tests of differences between means for each scale, since we are as much concerned with the characteristics of scales as with the characteristics of our sample. Whilst it would be misleading to suggest that multiple t-test results give an accurate picture of the extent of the differences between various groups, it is certainly the case that they give a good account of the characteristics of the individual *scale*.

The t-tests which follow in the various sections are two-tailed and adopt the conventional .05 probability level or beyond as the standard of statistical significance. Needless to say, with large groups of subjects statistical significance at this level may be based on relatively small differences in means and the reader should remember that the overlap between groups is often very substantial.

To overcome the problem of correlated scales we have also used Multiple Discriminant Analysis as a technique. Briefly stated, this involves essentially a factor analysis of the *differences* between a number of *groups* (rather than the *similarity* between questionnaire *items*), with an implied significance test of overall group differences. It allows us also to plot the inter-relationships between the various groups so as to present a graphical representation of these differences. The discriminant analyses we present were computed using a modified version of the program given by Overall and Klett (1972); an excellent description of the statisitical technique is also given by Tatsuoka (1972).

We shall therefore concern ourselves with three main types of differences: sex, discipline and cross-national. The reader should, of course, bear in mind that our findings are characteristics of our sample, and that an inferential step is needed if they are to be considered as characteristics of the whole undergraduate population: we do not have that most elusive of desirable properties, a perfect random sample, and the extent to which our findings reflect that population depends on the extent to which our sample approximates to the unattainable goal of randomness. However, given the size of the sample concerned, we have confidence in our results, particularly as compared with other studies with smaller, less widely sampled, poorly described or even indeterminate samples.

The one source of variability over which we had little control, *viz.* the image of the appointments service in each university, does, however, lead us to omit any discussion of the differences between the participating universities, on the grounds that such differences might well reflect sampling rather than population variability.

At this point we shall go into some detail on the method of presenting results in this and subsequent chapters. Confusion is most likely to arise with Cattell's Sixteen Personality Factor Questionnaire (16PF). We have already explained that approximately half the total sample took the parallel 16PF Forms A and B whilst the other half took the shorter 16PF Forms C and D with the addition of the IPAT Anxiety Scale (IAS), Neuroticism Scale Questionnaire (NSQ) and the Form A of the Eysenck Personality Inventory (EPI). These two subgroups we shall refer to as members of the 16PF A/B and 16PF C/D studies respectively. Some results on the 16PF are presented for each form separately in which case the actual form used will be clearly indicated in the relevant table. On other occasions, usually where overall tendencies are being discussed, factor scores have been summed across pairs of forms to gain scores on each factor based on two-form length; in this case reference will be made to Form A+B or alternatively Form C+D factor scores. It is important to remember that where the term Form A+B or Form C+D is used, it refers to the simple process of adding scale scores across the respective parallel forms — a procedure recommended by Cattell for greater reliability of factor measurement.

With 16PF second order factors there are further complications. As with the first order factors (primaries) scores have been obtained for each individual on Forms A,B and A+B or conversely Forms C,D and C+D. However, second orders are obtained first by converting the first orders to N-stens (the norm system used by Cattell based on a mean of 5.5 and a standard deviation of 2) and applying weights to these transformed scores. This calls into question the choice of suitable norm tables and the selection of the most appropriate weights.

Cattell (1970) has provided second order weights for both sexes combined but in general his separate weights for males and females were preferred in these analyses. For this reason, whilst the sexes may be compared in terms of their 16PF first order factor scores, no such comparison should be made on the eight 16PF second order factors or for that matter on the four derived criteria scales which are normed against separate sex norms.

On the problem of which norm groups to employ, there were no British student data readily available to use in converting the first order scales to second order factors, so because converted scores in N-sten units have a near perfect relationship with the original raw scores and as we were only concerned with differences between groups, in the absence of any real alternative, it was decided to use the American norms provided by Cattell (1972) as the basis for the conversion.

As a check, second orders Forms A and B were also normed against the British adult norms provided by Saville (1972) and whilst the units varied there were no important departures from the results given here. Once these decisions had been made, as with all the scoring, the second order factor and derived criteria scores were produced by computer: a necessary step in view of the million item responses and well over a quarter of a million scale scores which the study generated. Individual records were then classified by the various parameters described in the sections below and summary statistics calculated.

On the general plan of this chapter, each of the sections which follow on sex, discipline and cross national differences, contain means and standard deviations for the groups together with a test of significance between means. In addition to a short discussion at the end of these sections, a summary table giving the direction of significance differences is also presented.

Sex differences

In the present climate of opinion, the question of differences between the sexes, and the origin of such differences, is vexed to say the least. It seems to us, however, that there is a wealth of information in a survey such as this.

Personality differences on the 16PF first order factors between the British male and female undergraduate standardization samples for Forms A+B combined are given in Table 3.1. Thirteen of these differences are significant, males scoring higher on Factors C, E, H, L, Q1, Q2 and Q3 and females higher on Factors A, B, I, N, O and Q4, with no significant differences on F, G and M.

Table 3.2 gives the first order undergraduate sex differences on Forms C + D combined. Here males score higher on Factors E,F,L and Q1, and females are higher on Factors A,G,1,M,O and Q4. The remaining factors (B, C, H, N, Q2 and Q3) show non-significant differences in means.

Table 3.3 gives the consistency of the undergraduate sex differences across the forms of the 16PF. The higher scoring sex is given. The reader will remember that students were randomly assigned to the two studies (Forms A/B or Forms C/D) which were based on a counterbalanced questionnaire administration order. It is improbable, therefore, that the source of any variation across forms lies in the experimental design or sampling method.

It is not unreasonable to expect differences between the sexes in the variability of scores as well as in their means. Sign tests, which give the probability associated with a given set of differences, show that male undergraduates tend to yield higher standard deviations than females. This result is significant ($p. < 05$) on Forms A + B, but just fails to reach significance on Forms C + D. The interpretation of differences in variance is not always easy. There is a general feeling with tests of mental ability that the standard deviation of scores for males is higher than that for females. This has often been interpreted as showing that whilst on average there is no difference between mean IQs for males and females, the male sex tends to produce the geniuses and the idiots whereas women are more average!

There is, however, an alternative explanation available: quite simply it may be that test items, or even tests and the testing situation, may be more efficient at discriminating between men of different levels of ability than between women. Extending this argument to personality questionnaires, the apparently greater central tendency amongst women may be due either to the items being less relevant to their concerns and the salient features of their lives, or to a general tendency amongst

Table 3.1: Personality differences between British female and male undergraduates: 16PF Forms A + B combined

		A	B	C	E	F	G	H	I	L	M	N	O	Q1	Q2	Q3	Q4
British female undergraduates (N = 661)	*Mean*	20.31	18.60	29.70	21.91	30.13	22.07	22.76	26.80	15.64	27.36	18.75	25.78	19.90	19.83	20.49	28.77
	SD	6.58	2.75	7.11	7.72	8.56	6.51	11.39	5.89	5.30	6.09	4.65	7.94	5.91	6.08	6.58	9.32
British male undergraduates (N = 595)	*Mean*	17.96	18.23	31.09	27.20	29.61	21.64	24.40	20.35	17.50	27.50	17.63	21.12	21.52	20.59	22.20	24.30
	SD	6.92	2.94	7.60	7.58	9.39	6.69	11.95	6.87	5.40	6.54	4.52	8.69	5.58	6.22	6.69	9.59
Differences in means (positive if males higher)		−2.35	−.37	1.39	5.29	−.52	−.43	1.64	−6.45	2.06	.14	−1.12	−4.66	1.63	.76	1.71	−4.47
t value		6.16	2.30	3.34	12.22	1.02	1.15	2.48	17.89	6.81	.39	4.31	9.92	5.00	2.18	4.55	8.36
Significance of difference p<		.01	.05	.01	.01	NS	NS	.05	.01	.01	NS	.01	.01	.01	.05	.01	.01

Table 3.2: Personality differences between British female and male undergraduates: 16PF Forms C + D combined

		A	B	C	E	F	G	H	I	L	M	N	O	Q1	Q2	Q3	Q4
British female undergraduates (N = 669)	Mean	14.45	12.10	14.74	10.00	12.34	13.12	11.08	15.25	11.78	13.48	9.68	12.55	15.10	11.06	13.35	12.54
	SD	4.05	1.76	3.85	3.88	3.65	4.02	4.91	3.58	3.04	3.59	2.73	4.28	3.90	3.75	3.83	4.09
British male undergraduates (N = 587)	Mean	13.81	11.98	14.83	11.44	13.05	12.48	11.49	12.41	12.24	12.65	9.66	10.01	15.57	11.21	13.61	10.37
	SD	4.14	2.19	3.89	3.93	3.64	4.26	4.65	4.17	3.15	3.39	2.85	4.64	3.83	3.42	3.86	4.23
Differences in means (positive if males higher)		−.064	−.12	.09	1.44	.71	−.64	.41	−2.84	.46	−.83	−.02	−2.54	.47	.15	.26	−2.17
t value		2.76	1.07	.41	6.51	3.44	2.73	1.51	12.97	2.62	4.19	.12	10.08	2.14	.73	1.19	9.22
Significance of difference p<		.01	NS	NS	.01	.01	.01	NS	.01	.01	.01	NS	.01	.05	NS	NS	.01

Table 3.3: Significantly Higher Sex for Each Form of the 16PF: British Undergraduates

	A	B	C	E	F	G	H	I	L	M	N	O	Q1	Q2	Q3	Q4	
Form A	F**	NS	M*	M**	F*	NS	M*	F**	M**	NS	F**	F**	M**	NS	M**	F**	
Form B	F**	F**	M**	M**	NS	F**	M*	F**	M**	NS	NS	F**	NS	M**	M**	F**	
Forms A + B	F**	F*	M**	M**	NS	NS	M*	F**	M**	NS	F**	F**	M**	M*	M**	F**	Forms A + B standardization sample
Form C	NS	NS	NS	M**	NS	F*	NS	F**	NS	F**	NS	F**	NS	NS	M**	F**	
Form D	F**	NS	NS	M*	M**	F*	NS	F**	M**	F**	NS	F**	M**	NS	NS	F**	
Forms C + D	F**	NS	NS	M**	M**	F**	NS	F**	M**	F**	NS	F**	M*	NS	NS	F**	Forms C + D standardization sample

F: Female significantly higher scoring sex
M: Male significantly higher scoring sex

** p < .01
* p < .05

women to be more cautious and express less extreme opinions, rather than to any real difference in the actual parameters which go to make up personality. One might expect this smaller variance to be reflected in lower reliability coefficients, by analogy with the restricted range phenomenon.

Table 3.4 gives the sex differences for the IAS, NSQ and EPI scales. Female students scored higher than males on all factors in the IAS and NSQ (with the sole exception of Factor L in the IAS) and on the total scores for both these questionnaires. On the EPI, there is a significant difference on the Neuroticism Scale, females scoring higher.

A comparison between sex differences in undergraduates and general population adults

It is possible to investigate not only the extent to which male and female undergraduates differ but also the extent to which such differences reflect differences in the population as a whole. A study standardizing the 16PF on British adults was undertaken by Saville (1972) and the results for male and female adults are summarized in Table 3.5.

We find, in fact, that as regards the 16PF Forms A + B, the differences reported by Saville (1972) hold with the single exception of Factor B (Summary Table 3.6.). In the general population a slight, but statistically significant, difference was found between the scores of males and females on the intelligence factor, women scoring slightly lower.

In the undergraduate population, this effect appears to be reversed. However, it seems to us likely that this effect is attributable to the more highly selected nature of female as opposed to male undergraduates: since scholastic ability is presumably one of the variables contributing to the selection of undergraduates, and since fewer undergraduate places are given to women than to men, what we see here may be the effect of 'creaming' by the universities. In fact, the effect is relatively slight, and only becomes significant on Form B. Therefore, we hesitate to impose too great a burden of interpretation on it.

Amongst the other differences, some, such as the higher mean score for males on Factor E, tend to confirm the social stereotype of the male as tending to be more dominant that the female; similarly, the differences on Factors C, 1, 0 and Q4 suggesting that women are more tender-minded and emotionally labile, more open to anxiety, and frustration, may well be taken as confirming popular belief. The male chauvinist might also point to the difference on Factor N as indicating the shrewdness and guile of womankind as opposed to straightforward, open, artless man!

Table 3.4: Personality differences between British female and male undergraduates on the IAS, NSQ and EPI

		IPAT Anxiety Scale						Neuroticism Scale Questionaire					Eysenck Personality Inventory	
		Q3	C	L	O	Q4	Total	I	F	E	An	Total	E	N
Female Undergraduates N = 668	Mean	7.28	4.45	3.38	10.81	8.69	34.62	12.31	8.57	11.68	10.45	43.01	11.42	11.00
	SD	2.72	2.14	1.67	3.39	3.61	9.88	2.81	3.15	3.04	3.09	6.96	4.27	4.92
Male Undergraduates N = 585	Mean	7.01	4.19	3.82	8.83	7.80	31.66	10.06	8.33	9.44	9.77	37.60	11.44	9.08
	SD	2.77	2.15	1.70	3.71	3.63	10.28	3.45	3.33	3.13	3.44	7.92	4.52	4.96
Difference in means (Positive if male undergraduates higher)		−.27	−.26	.44	−1.98	−.89	−2.96	−2.25	−.24	−2.24	−.68	−5.41	0.02	−1.92
t value		1.74	2.14	4.61	9.86	4.34	5.19	12.70	1.30	12.82	3.68	12.86	0.08	6.86
Significance of difference p<		NS	.05	.01	.01	.01	.01	.01	NS	.01	.01	.01	NS	.01

Table 3.5: Personality differences between British female and male adults: 16PF Forms A + B

		A	B	C	E	F	G	H	I	L	M	N	O	Q1	Q2	Q3	Q4
Female	Mean	21.72	14.16	28.07	19.09	26.42	24.79	23.48	25.01	15.89	21.75	22.34	25.35	16.49	19.68	28.13	28.78
	SD	5.02	3.44	6.67	6.69	8.61	5.46	10.36	4.58	4.94	5.92	4.71	7.58	4.71	5.59	5.73	8.16
Male	Mean	17.58	14.65	30.80	25.00	26.27	24.63	27.25	17.63	17.72	22.94	20.96	19.69	18.86	20.40	24.86	23.77
	SD	5.85	3.47	6.99	7.30	9.23	5.90	10.30	5.76	4.95	5.63	4.80	7.79	4.97	5.76	6.00	9.20
Difference in means (Positive if female higher)		−4.14	0.49	2.73	5.91	−0.15	−0.16	3.77	−7.38	1.83	1.19	−1.38	−5.66	2.37	0.72	1.73	−5.01
t value		17.02	3.18	8.96	18.92	0.38	0.63	8.18	31.78	8.29	4.62	6.50	16.50	10.97	2.84	6.61	12.91
Significance of difference $p<$		.001	.01	.01	.001	NS	NS	.001	.001	.001	.001	.001	.001	.001	.01	.001	.001

(Reproduced from Saville, 1972)

Interestingly, although differences between male and female undergraduates are in the same direction as those between males and females in the general population, the absolute size of the differences tends to be smaller. That is to say, although on average undergraduates of either sex differ in the same respects, they are less different than the population as a whole. Perhaps it is to be expected that the scholastic achievement and the motivation necessary to carry the individual over the various hurdles of educational selection will result in undergraduates of either sex being rather more similar in personality than unselected groups. On the other hand one might wish to argue that the fact that such large differences remain even in such a selected group is indicative of the abiding significance of sex differences.

Discipline differences in 16PF first order factors

How far is the traditional distinction between arts and sciences reflected in different scores on personality scales? There has long been held an opinion that choice of specialization is associated with more than mere occupational preference: Hudson's work on convergent and divergent thinking in English schoolboys (Hudson, 1972) is illustrative of the interest provoked by the division.

In the present study, respondents were asked to indicate the principal subject in their degree course, i.e. essentially the question was put: 'What are you reading?' Their answers, coded into the nine categories used by the university Grants Committee (See page 33), were cross-checked when data on degree results were added, and means and standard deviations calculated for each form of the questionnaires by sex.

The results of t-tests on these data are presented in Tables 3.7 to 3.10. Since within our sample there is a relationship between sex and discipline, data for both sexes combined within one discipline will tend to reflect the sex differences reported above: that is to say, since fewer women study the sciences and technological subjects, the composition of our sample is correspondingly biased.

Under the general heading 'Science' we include Medicine, Engineering and Technology, Agriculture and Forestry and the Physical and Biological Sciences, whilst 'Arts' includes Social Sciences, Professional and Vocational subjects, Language, Literature and Area studies, Education and 'other arts'. The inclusion of social sciences in the arts category was decided on after inspection of the data, when it became clear that the mean scores for social science students were much closer to those of arts students than to those of science students.

There are, it is clear, a number of significant differences in mean scale scores for the two disciplines, most strikingly in the case of Factor I (Tough v Tender-Mindedness).

Table 3.6: Comparison of the sex differences found with British undergraduates with those of British adults: 16PF Forms A + B

	A	B	C	E	F	G	H	I	L	M	N	O	Q1	Q2	Q3	Q4
British undergraduates: higher scoring sex	F**	F*	M**	M**	NS	NS	M*	F**	M**	NS	F**	F**	M**	M*	M**	F**
British adults: higher scoring sex	F**	M**	M**	M**	NS	NS	M**	F**	M**	M**	F**	F**	M**	M**	M**	F**

M: Male significantly higher scoring sex
F: Female significantly higher scoring sex

* p<.05
** p<.01

Table 3.7: Personality differences between arts and science undergraduates: female: 16PF First order factors:

Forms A + B combined

	A	B	C	E	F	G	H	I	L	M	N	O	Q1	Q2	Q3	Q4
Female science (N = 224) mean	18.19	18.56	31.17	21.30	29.93	22.94	22.66	23.22	15.02	25.93	18.54	25.04	19.20	19.33	21.50	27.85
SD	6.74	2.84	6.85	7.39	8.90	6.59	11.29	5.86	5.04	5.86	4.59	7.73	5.60	5.92	6.09	9.10
Female arts (N = 437) mean	21.39	18.62	28.95	22.23	30.24	21.63	22.81	28.64	15.96	28.10	18.86	26.17	20.27	20.09	19.98	29.25
SD	6.23	2.70	7.13	7.87	8.39	6.44	11.46	5.01	5.41	6.09	4.69	8.03	6.03	6.14	6.77	9.41
Differences in means (positive if science higher)	−3.20	.06	2.22	−.93	−.31	1.31	−.15	−5.42	−.94	−2.17	−.32	−1.13	−1.07	−.76	1.52	−1.40
t value	6.06	.27	3.83	1.47	.44	2.45	.16	12.39	2.16	4.39	.84	1.73	2.21	1.52	2.82	1.83
Significance of difference p <	.01	NS	.01	NS	NS	.01	NS	.01	.05	.01	NS	NS	.05	NS	.01	NS

Table 3.8: Personality differences between arts and science undergraduates: female: 16PF First order factors: Forms C + D combined

	A	B	C	E	F	G	H	I	L	M	N	O	Q1	Q2	Q3	Q4
Female science (N = 238) *mean*	13.63	12.20	15.05	10.00	12.50	13.53	10.73	13.57	11.35	12.36	9.74	12.09	14.44	10.87	13.95	12.26
SD	3.94	1.82	3.91	3.71	3.35	3.91	4.72	3.24	2.92	3.40	2.79	4.15	3.78	3.49	3.68	4.06
Female arts (N = 427) *mean*	14.90	12.04	14.53	10.05	12.27	12.92	11.30	16.19	12.04	14.14	9.63	12.82	15.51	11.18	13.01	12.70
SD	4.30	1.74	3.80	3.97	3.82	4.03	4.98	3.43	3.09	3.54	2.71	4.31	3.91	3.89	3.87	4.08
Differences in means (positive if science higher)	−1.27	.16	.52	−.05	.23	.61	−.57	−2.62	−.69	−1.78	.11	−.73	−1.07	−.31	.94	−.44
t value	3.76	1.12	1.67	.16	.78	1.89	1.44	9.62	2.81	6.29	.49	2.12	3.42	1.02	3.05	1.33
Significance of difference p<	.01	NS	NS	NS	NS	NS	NS	.01	.01	.01	NS	.05	.01	NS	.01	NS

Table 3.9: Personality differences between arts and science undergraduates: male: 16PF First order factors: Forms A + B combined

	A	B	C	E	F	G	H	I	L	M	N	O	Q1	Q2	Q3	Q4
Male science (N = 337) *mean*	15.57	18.40	31.83	26.44	28.56	21.71	22.82	18.10	16.96	26.90	17.82	20.91	20.99	20.92	22.82	23.67
SD	6.20	2.84	7.14	7.70	8.93	6.68	11.45	6.39	5.39	6.41	4.24	8.49	5.49	5.89	6.42	9.28
Male arts (N = 255) *mean*	21.12	18.00	30.19	28.28	31.06	21.51	26.58	23.35	18.72	28.36	17.34	21.34	22.32	20.18	21.37	25.11
SD	6.57	3.04	8.04	7.28	9.83	6.72	12.26	6.37	5.28	6.63	4.85	8.92	5.61	6.61	6.97	9.98
Differences in means (positive if science higher)	−5.55	.40	1.64	−1.84	−2.50	.20	−3.76	−5.25	−1.76	−1.46	.48	−.43	−1.33	.74	1.45	−1.44
t value	10.49	1.64	2.62	2.94	3.22	.36	3.83	9.90	3.96	2.70	1.28	.60	2.89	1.43	2.62	1.81
Significance of difference p <	.01	NS	.01	.01	.01	NS	.01	.01	.01	.01	NS	NS	.01	NS	.01	NS

Table 3.10: Personality differences between arts and science undergraduates: male: 16PF First order factors: Forms C + D combined

	A	B	C	E	F	G	H	I	L	M	N	O	Q1	Q2	Q3	Q4
Male science (N = 330) *mean*	12.73	12.05	15.05	11.45	13.17	12.51	11.14	11.25	12.30	12.08	9.51	9.64	15.23	10.95	13.82	9.98
SD	4.16	2.21	3.85	3.92	3.60	4.26	4.76	3.71	3.13	3.32	2.90	4.65	3.89	3.55	3.84	4.03
Male arts (N = 252) *mean*	15.25	11.88	14.57	11.40	12.36	12.43	11.94	13.97	12.16	13.39	9.85	10.47	16.05	11.55	13.33	10.88
SD	3.69	2.17	3.95	3.97	3.72	4.26	4.49	4.22	3.16	3.35	2.80	4.62	3.71	3.23	3.88	4.45
Differences in means (positive if science higher)	−2.52	.17	.48	.05	.81	.80	−.08	−2.72	.14	−1.31	−.34	−.83	−.82	−.60	.49	−.90
t value	7.59	.93	1.47	.15	2.65	.22	2.06	8.24	.53	4.69	1.42	2.14	2.57	2.10	1.52	2.55
Significance of difference $p <$	.01	NS	NS	NS	.01	NS	.05	.01	NS	.01	NS	.05	.01	.05	NS	.05

The difference in mean scores for both males and females taken separately, between arts and science specialists is not far short of one standard deviation on Forms A + B combined. Such a difference is large indeed, and given the large size of the samples concerned, very highly statistically significant. Furthermore, the figures we present mask even greater differences between certain of the groups: for instance, the difference in mean scores on Factor I between male linguists and male engineers is about 10 raw score points, that is to say, not much less than two standard deviations.

It is instructive to examine the individual items which make up the Factor I scales in the 16PF and note how many of them relate to occupational interests in the broadest sense — aesthetic preference as well as career preference. Perhaps even more interestingly, Factor I is described in terms of 'Tough-mindedness—Tender-mindedness', a label identical with that employed by Eysenck (1954) to describe a 'social attitude', and more recently 'psychoticism'.

Other factors on which consistent differences are found across forms are: A (arts more outgoing), L (arts more Suspicious), M (arts more Imaginative), Q1 (arts more Radical) and Q3 (science more socially precise and controlled). Amongst these, only Factor A is a major contributor to the second order Exvia factor, and none of the three most important contributors to Anxiety (C, O, Q4) is present. And in Factor Q1 we have yet another factor which carries the same description as one of Eysenck's social attitudes (Conservatism—Radicalism). Here is some evidence then that the 16PF primaries have consistent descriptive power in areas not obviously covered by the EPI.

Amongst the 16 factors, only B (Intelligence) and N (Shrewdness) show no differences at all between the disciplines. There are, however, a number of inconsistencies across forms on a number of the other factors (Table 3.11). For example, there is a significant difference between the disciplines on Factor C Forms A and B, but not on Forms C and D. However, with Factor O the situation is reversed, there being a significant difference only on Forms C and D. Given the first of these differences, one might be tempted to suppose that the shortness of the Forms C and D scales is responsible for the difference not reaching statistical significance. However, this cannot be the case with Factor O, since here it is the forms with the shorter scales which exhibit the difference; one must therefore conclude that this anomaly has its roots in item content.

In summary, there are significant differences in mean scores between the disciplines, which are almost exclusively in the same direction for both sexes, although there are inconsistencies across forms. (See summary Table 3.11.) This is not to say, however, that the sex

Table 3.11: Personality differences between academic disciplines: Summary Table: 16PF First order factors

	A	B	C	E	F	G	H	I	L	M	N	O	Q1	Q2	Q3	Q4
Females A+B	AT	NS	SC	NS	NS	SC	NS	AT	AT	AT	NS	NS	AT	NS	SC	NS
Females C+D	AT	NS	NS	NS	NS	NS	NS	AT	AT	AT	NS	AT	AT	NS	SC	NS
Males A+B	AT	NS	SC	AT	AT	NS	AT	AT	AT	AT	NS	NS	AT	NS	SC	NS
Males C+D	AT	NS	NS	NS	SC	NS	AT	AT	NS	AT	NS	AT	AT	AT	NS	AT

AT: Arts Undergraduates significantly higher
SC: Science Undergraduates significantly higher

differences and discipline differences are in the same direction; some are and others are not. Clearly, to understand the scores of undergraduates we must take both sex and discipline into account. The question of the interaction of sex and discipline could be pursued using analysis of variance techniques. To some extent this approach is implicit in the multiple discriminant analysis described later in this chapter.

Discipline differences in 16PF second order factors and derived criteria

Tables 3.12 to 3.15 present the corresponding data for the 16PF Second Order Factors. We should add one note of warning concerning these second order data. The means and standard deviations given in Tables 3.12 to 3.15 are expressed in American General Population N-sten units derived from the separate male and female norm tables and scoring weights provided by Cattell (1970). No comparisons should be made, therefore, between the sexes on the second order factors or derived criteria.

Male arts students score significantly higher on Exvia on Forms A + B, but not female arts students and not male arts students on Forms C + D. On Anxiety arts students score significantly higher, with the single exception of males on Forms A + B. The other second order factors show no consistent pattern: the deviant behaviour of QVI (Prodigal Subjectivity) suggests that something is amiss. It is quite extraordinary that the mean scores for well-defined criterion groups should have the precise opposite relationship depending on whether they are calculated from Form A + B or Form C + D scales.

As for the 'derived criteria', males on Forms A + B show no significant differences at all. Arts students score higher on Cattell's Neuroticism but perhaps more intriguingly scientists score higher on Leadership and arts specialists on Creativity.

Since employers commonly look to science graduates for creative innovation and to arts graduates for managerial leadership, we must ask whether there is something singular about the concepts as employed by Cattell, or whether in fact these results reflect the true state of affairs using the terms in their common acceptance.

Discipline differences in the EPI, IAS and NSQ scales

The discipline differences on the EPI, IAS and NSQ are given in Tables 3.17 and 3.18. The EPI factors show no significant differences between the disciplines for males but female arts are significantly more Neurotic than female science students.

On the NSQ, arts students score higher, both males and females, whereas on the IAS there is no significant difference for females, but male arts students score higher. These results are congruent with the results for the corresponding scales in the 16PF.

Table 3.12: Personality differences between British arts and science undergraduates: female: 16PF Forms A + B combined: Second order factors and derived criteria

| | Second order factor | | | | | | | | | Derived criteria | | |
	Exvia QI	Anxiety QII	Cortertia $QIII$	Independence QIV	Discreetness QV	Prodigal subjectivity QVI	Intelligence $QVII$	Super ego strength $QVIII$	Neuroticism	Leadership	Creativity	School achievement
Female Arts undergraduates (N = 396) *Mean*	5.48	6.09	5.07	6.99	4.38	6.18	8.04	3.91	5.63	4.74	7.31	6.08
SD	2.03	1.91	2.09	2.03	2.07	1.96	1.62	2.07	1.85	1.77	1.87	1.90
Female science undergraduates (N = 302) *Mean*	5.31	5.70	5.67	6.29	4.14	4.47	8.09	4.30	4.97	5.32	6.70	5.78
SD	2.13	1.83	1.87	1.87	1.97	2.07	1.73	2.08	1.87	1.74	1.89	1.83
Differences in means (positive if arts higher)	.17	.39	-.60	.70	.24	1.71	-.05	-.39	.66	-.58	.61	.30
t value	.95	2.39	3.44	4.09	1.36	9.90	.35	2.18	4.11	3.81	3.76	1.85
Significance of difference $p <$	NS	.01	.01	.01	NS	.01	NS	.05	.01	.01	.01	NS

Table 3.13: Personality differences between British arts and science undergraduates: female: 16PF Forms C + D combined: Second order factors and derived criteria

		Second order factors							Derived criteria			
		Exvia QI	Anxiety QII	Corter-tia QIII	Indepen-dence QIV	Discreet-ness QV	Prodigal subject-ivity QVI	Intell-igence QVII	Super ego str-engtb QVIII	Neurot-icism	Leader-ship	Creati-vity	School achieve-ment
Female arts undergrad-uates (N = 389)	Mean	5.01	5.71	6.73	4.67	5.87	4.76	7.08	6.14	6.11	4.44	7.50	6.40
	SD	1.36	1.95	1.40	1.55	1.57	1.43	1.63	1.58	1.73	1.60	1.74	1.57
Female science undergrad-uates (N = 220)	Mean	5.14	4.76	6.86	5.00	5.36	5.26	6.57	5.93	5.55	5.00	6.98	6.33
	SD	1.30	1.68	1.45	1.55	1.42	1.42	1.51	1.55	1.56	1.52	1.66	1.58
Differences in means (positive if arts higher)		−.13	.95	−.13	−.33	.51	−.50	.51	.21	.56	−.56	.52	.07
t value		1.15	6.05	1.08	2.52	3.98	4.15	3.80	1.58	3.97	4.22	3.60	.53
Significance of difference p <		NS	.01	NS	.01	.01	.01	.01	NS	.01	.01	.01	NS

Table 3.14: Personality differences between British arts and science undergraduates: male: 16PF Forms A + B combined: Second order factors and derived criteria

		Second order factors									Derived criteria		
		Exvia QI	*Anxiety* QII	*Cortertia* QIII	*Independence* QIV	*Discreetness* QV	*Prodigal subjectivity* QVI	*Intelligence* QVII	*Superego strength* QVIII	*Neuroticism*	*Leadership*	*Creativity*	*School achievement*
Male arts undergraduates (N = 235)	*Mean*	5.47	6.45	4.92	6.84	4.36	6.67	7.82	3.79	6.09	4.38	7.36	6.15
	SD	2.32	2.05	2.15	2.13	2.25	2.10	1.80	2.12	2.25	2.11	2.04	1.98
Male science undergraduates (N = 314)	*Mean*	4.72	6.21	6.68	6.44	4.55	6.04	7.95	3.94	5.82	4.50	7.33	6.12
	SD	2.15	1.87	1.98	2.12	1.98	2.17	1.68	2.08	2.06	1.96	1.88	2.01
Differences in means (positive if arts higher)		.75	.24	−1.76	.40	−.19	.63	−.13	−.15	.27	−.12	.03	.03
t value		3.90	1.42	9.91	2.18	1.05	3.41	.87	.83	1.46	.69	.18	.17
Significance of difference p <		.01	NS	.01	.05	NS	.01	NS	NS	NS	NS	NS	NS

Table 3.15: Personality differences between British arts and science undergraduates: male: 16PF Forms C + D combined. Second order factors and derived criteria

	Second order factors								Derived Criteria			
	Exvia QI	Anxiety QII	Cortertia QIII	Independence QIV	Discreetness QV	Prodigal subjectivity QVI	Intelligence QVII	Super ego strengtb QVIII	Neuroticism	Leadership	Creativity	School achievement.
Male arts undergraduates (N = 237) Mean	5.18	6.82	6.81	4.79	6.14	4.55	6.88	6.26	6.16	4.45	7.13	6.41
SD	1.57	1.91	1.67	1.59	1.71	1.43	1.63	1.72	1.82	1.56	1.76	1.79
Male science undergraduates (N = 312) Mean	5.05	6.02	6.79	4.63	5.51	4.85	6.45	5.75	5.53	4.85	6.79	6.20
SD	1.57	1.66	1.63	1.67	1.52	1.37	1.62	1.73	1.80	1.59	1.72	1.79
Differences in means (positive if arts higher)	.13	.80	.02	.16	.63	−.30	.43	.51	.63	−.40	.34	.21
t value	.95	5.23	.14	1.13	4.55	2.49	3.07	3.42	4.04	2.94	2.27	1.36
Significance of difference p <	NS	.01	NS	NS	.01	.01	.01	.01	.01	.01	.05	NS

Table 3.16: Personality differences between academic disciplines: Summary Table: 16PF second order factors and derived criteria.

	Second order factors								Derived criteria			
	Exvia	Anxiety	Cortertia	Independence	Discreetness	Prodigal subjectivity	Intelligence	Superego strength	Neuroticism	Leadership	Creativity	School achievement
	QI	QII	QIII	QIV	QV	QVI	QVII	QVIII				
Females A+B	NS	AT**	SC**	AT**	NS	AT**	NS	SC*	AT**	SC**	AT**	NS
Females C+D	NS	AT**	NS	SC**	AT**	SC**	AT**	NS	AT**	SC**	AT**	NS
Males A+B	AT**	NS	SC*	AT*	NS	AT**	NS	NS	NS	NS	NS	NS
Males C+D	NS	AT**	NS	NS	AT**	SC**	AT**	AT**	AT**	SC**	AT*	NS

AT: Arts Students Significantly Higher.
SC: Science Students Significantly Higher.

* p<.05
** p<.01

Table 3.17: Personality differences between arts and science undergraduates: female: IAS, NSQ, and EPI

		IAS Total	NSQ Total	Eysenck Personality Inventory E	N
Female science students (N = 238)	*Mean*	33.72	41.69	11.42	10.46
	SD	9.91	6.91	4.14	4.78
Female arts students (N = 426)	*Mean*	35.20	43.77	11.42	11.34
	SD	9.79	6.89	4.34	4.97
Difference in means (positive if science higher)		−1.48	−2.08	0	−.88
t value		1.86	3.72	0	2.21
Significance of difference p <		NS	.01	NS	.05

Table 3.18: Personality differences between arts and science undergraduates: Male: IAS, NSQ and EPI

		IAS Total	NSQ Total	Eysenck Personality Inventory E	N
Male science students (N = 329)	*Mean*	30.68	36.14	11.26	8.77
	SD	9.92	7.85	4.45	4.89
Male arts students (N = 251)	*Mean*	32.73	39.55	11.64	9.45
	SD	10.63	7.62	4.62	5.07
Difference in means (positive if science higher)		−2.05	−3.41	−.38	−.68
t value		2.39	5.24	1.00	1.63
Significance of difference p <		.05	.01	NS	NS

Multiple discriminant analyses

Once the univariate comparisons discussed above were completed, it became clear that a further step was needed. There was no doubt that significant differences do exist between the sexes and disciplines in terms of mean scale scores. However, given the extent to which the scales are correlated amongst themselves, the possibility remained that the extent of the differences was exaggerated. Thus, it was decided to undertake discriminant analysis of the data with reference to sex and discipline.

Discriminant analysis involves the computation of linear combinations of scores weighted so as to discriminate maximally amongst the various groups involved.

The particular technique employed is described by Overall and Klett (1972) and is distinctive in that the functions obtained are orthogonal 'factors', unlike other variants of multiple discriminant analysis. Implicit in the computational procedures is a test of significance for each successive factor extracted.

The use of multiple discriminant analysis simplifies the analysis of differences between groups by concentrating on the between-groups variance, provides a multivariate test of significance of differences and allows a reduction in the number of dimensions to be considered.

The analysis was first carried out on the 16PF Forms A and B data, using course code, i.e. the UGC nine-point classification, as the basis of the analysis. A few of the groups containing only a handful of subjects, e.g. females doing professional and vocational subjects, had to be dropped for this purpose.

Figure 3.1 is a plot of course code groups by sex against the first two discriminant functions, which together account for more than 75 per cent of the variation in the matrix. The points plotted represent the mean score for each group on each discriminant function. It is plain that the course codes used cluster into four groupings which we may label male arts, male science, female arts and female science. Female engineers are the only group at all deviant in this clustering, and they are few in number. The analysis was then repeated, using these clusters as the new group variables, and the 32 scales in Forms A and B of the 16PF scored separately rather than added across forms. Results are plotted in Figure 3.2. Only two functions were obtained in this analysis.

The principal scales contributing to the discrimination are, for the first function, I, A, E, O and Q4. Of these, I (Tough v. Tender-mindedness) is far and away the most important. The second discriminant function has contributions largely from Factors A, E, I, M, O, Q1 and Q4 on Form A, and A, E, H and O on Form B.

Since discriminant functions are factors, they may, like factors, be

Figure 3.1: Plot of course code by discriminant functions 1 and 2
16PF Form A + B Combined

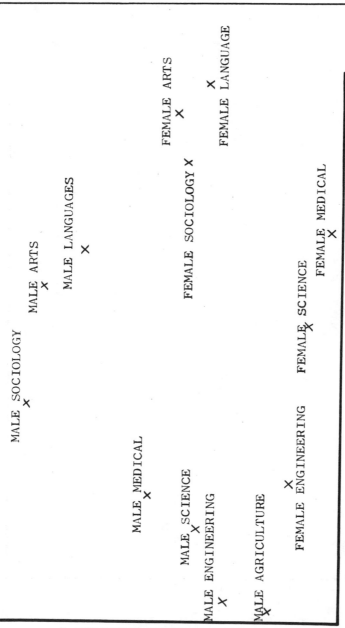

**Figure 3.2: Plot of discipline by discriminant functions 1 and 2
16PF Form A + B Combined**

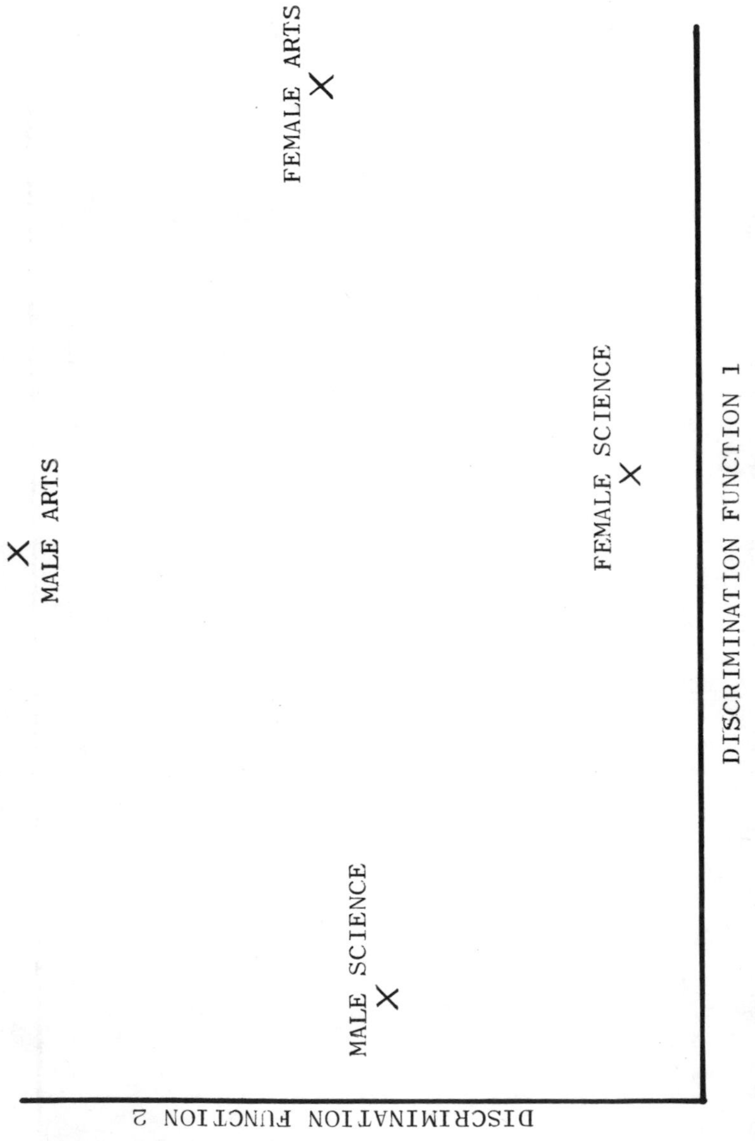

FEMALE ARTS
×

FEMALE SCIENCE
×

DISCRIMINATION FUNCTION 1

MALE ARTS
×

MALE SCIENCE
×

DISCRIMINATION FUNCTION 2

rotated so as to be more easily named. It is clear that these two functions could be rotated so as to obtain one loading sex and the other discipline, with a degree of obliqueness, i.e. correlation, between the two. The implication of this is that one could derive from 16PF scales specification equations to predict the sex and discipline of an individual, but one can think of more obvious ways of extracting this information.

Other analyses of the data for both pairs of forms have been carried out using the same methods, but different combinations of scales and groupings: the results presented here are representative and presentation of further data or plottings would be merely repetitious. No significant deviations from these findings have been obtained.

Cross national differences between American college and British university students

Differences between the British undergraduate and American college students are given in Tables 3.19 to 3.24. For females across Forms A + B combined and C + D combined British students are consistently lower on Factors A, F, G, H, N and Q3, and higher on B, M, Q1 and Q2. Similarly British male undergraduates are consistently higher than male American students on factors B, I, M, Q1 and Q2 and lower on A, F, G, H and Q4.

In general terms then, British undergraduates would appear more reserved (A−), Intelligent (B+), Sober (F−), Expedient (G−), Shy (H−), Imaginative (M+), Experimenting (Q1+) and Self-sufficient (Q2+) than their American counterparts.

The proverbial reserve, sobriety and self-sufficiency of the British would seem to be the clearest finding here. Once more the difference on Factor B is most probably to be attributed to the greater degree of selection practised in Great Britain as opposed to the USA. Only some eight to ten per cent of young Britons attend university, whereas in America college entrance is a much more open system. Furthermore, there is a clear distinction in Great Britain between universities and other types of tertiary education: hence the British university population will tend to be in the highest ability range. We thus advise against any strong conclusions being drawn from this difference as to the relative levels of ability in the two nations.

Summary

From the point of view of those involved in student welfare in higher education, the discipline differences we have found are clearly important. From our data, it would seem that arts students are more outgoing and radical, whilst science students are more conservative and socially controlled. It is impossible to estimate whether these

Table 3.19: Personality differences between American college students and British undergraduates: female: 16PF Forms A + B combined

		A	B	C	E	F	G	H	I	L	M	N	O	Q1	Q2	Q3	Q4
British female undergraduates N = 661	Mean	20.31	18.60	29.70	21.91	30.13	22.07	22.76	26.80	15.64	27.36	18.75	25.78	19.90	19.83	20.49	28.77
	SD	6.58	2.75	7.11	7.72	8.56	6.51	11.39	5.89	5.30	6.09	4.65	7.94	5.91	6.08	6.58	9.32
American female college students N = 1182	Mean	22.98	17.50	31.19	22.56	33.32	25.33	26.66	26.66	15.51	25.24	19.66	23.16	17.17	16.94	22.18	23.26
	SD	6.04	2.94	7.10	7.30	7.96	5.99	11.07	5.18	5.22	6.49	4.32	7.67	5.11	5.98	5.96	3.65
Differences in means (positive if British higher)		−2.67	1.10	−1.49	−.65	−3.19	−3.26	−3.90	.15	.13	2.12	−.91	2.62	2.73	2.89	−1.69	.51
t value		8.80	7.87	4.31	1.79	8.02	19.85	7.17	.56	.50	6.87	4.21	6.94	10.38	9.88	5.61	1.17
Significance of difference p <		.01	.01	.01	NS	.01	.01	.01	NS	NS	.01	.01	.01	.01	.01	.01	NS

Table 3.20: Personality differences between American college students and British undergraduates; female: 16PF Forms C + D combined

		A	B	C	E	F	G	H	I	L	M	N	O	Q1	Q2	Q3	Q4
British female undergraduates N = 669	Mean	14.45	12.10	14.74	10.00	12.34	13.12	11.08	15.25	11.78	13.48	9.68	12.55	15.10	11.06	13.35	12.54
	SD	4.05	1.76	3.85	3.88	3.65	4.02	4.91	3.58	3.04	3.59	2.73	4.28	3.90	3.75	3.83	4.09
American female college students N = 1031	Mean	15.26	10.94	13.97	9.60	14.17	14.67	12.12	14.33	13.06	11.45	10.48	13.84	13.39	8.34	13.98	12.78
	SD	4.16	2.17	4.63	3.94	4.03	4.21	5.19	3.49	3.44	3.75	3.22	4.73	4.17	3.96	4.03	4.63
Differences in means (positive if British higher)		−.81	1.16	.77	.40	−1.83	−1.55	−1.04	.92	−1.28	2.03	−.80	−1.29	1.71	2.72	−.63	−.24
t value		3.96	11.57	3.57	2.06	9.48	7.54	4.12	5.25	7.84	11.08	5.30	5.70	8.47	14.12	3.21	1.09
Significance of difference p <		.01	.01	.01	.05	.01	.01	.01	.01	.01	.01	.01	.01	.01	.01	.01	.05

Table 3.21— Personality differences between American college students and British undergraduates: male: 16PF Forms A + B combined

		A	B	C	E	F	G	H	I	L	M	N	O	Q1	Q2	Q3	Q4
British male undergraduates N = 595	Mean	17.96	18.23	31.09	27.20	29.61	21.64	24.40	20.35	17.70	27.50	17.63	21.12	21.53	20.59	22.20	24.30
	SD	6.92	2.94	7.60	7.58	9.39	6.69	11.95	6.87	5.40	6.54	4.52	8.69	5.58	6.22	6.69	9.59
American male college students N = 1517	Mean	19.72	17.50	31.36	27.89	32.34	24.27	27.45	17.71	17.83	24.79	17.80	20.57	19.91	18.30	22.64	25.75
	SD	6.92	2.94	7.19	7.11	8.28	6.25	10.96	6.46	5.19	6.79	4.26	7.91	5.26	6.26	5.60	8.63
Differences in means (positive if British higher)		−1.76	.73	−.27	−.69	−2.73	−2.63	−3.05	2.64	−.13	2.71	−.17	.55	1.62	2.29	−.44	−1.45
t value		5.25	5.13	.76	1.96	6.55	8.52	5.60	8.29	.51	8.33	.81	1.39	6.25	7.57	1.53	3.36
Significance of difference P <		.01	.01	NS	.05	.01	.01	.01	.01	NS	.01	NS	NS	.01	.01	NS	.01

Table 3.22: Personality differences between American college students and British undergraduates: Male: 16PF Forms C + D combined

		A	B	C	E	F	G	H	I	L	M	N	O	Q1	Q2	Q3	Q4
British male undergraduates N = 587	Mean	13.81	11.98	14.83	11.44	13.05	12.48	11.49	12.41	12.24	12.65	9.66	10.01	15.57	11.21	13.61	10.37
	SD	4.41	2.19	3.89	3.93	3.64	4.26	4.65	4.17	3.15	3.39	2.85	4.46	3.83	3.42	3.86	4.23
American male college students N = 930	Mean	14.33	10.66	14.43	11.47	14.19	13.73	12.51	10.75	13.43	11.00	10.25	11.84	14.14	9.43	14.14	11.07
	SD	4.22	2.20	4.37	3.88	3.93	4.30	5.13	4.30	3.25	3.62	3.03	4.79	3.95	3.94	3.79	4.33
Differences in means (positive if British higher)		−.52	1.32	.40	−.03	−1.14	−1.25	−1.02	1.66	−1.19	1.65	−.59	−1.83	1.43	1.78	−.53	−.70
t value		2.35	11.39	1.80	.14	5.65	5.53	3.90	7.40	7.02	8.85	3.77	7.33	6.94	9.00	2.63	3.09
Significance of difference $p <$		.05	.01	NS	NS	.01	.01	.01	.01	.01	.01	.01	.01	.01	.01	.01	.01

Table 3.23: Personality differences between American college students and British undergraduates: the IPAT Anxiety Scale

	Females		Males		Females + Males	
	Mean	*SD*	*Mean*	*SD*	*Mean*	*SD*
British undergraduates N = 668 / 585 / 1256	34.62	9.88	31.66	10.28	33.22	10.17
American college students N = 555 / 837 / 1392	29.70	10.20	27.70	10.10	28.70	10.40
Differences in mean (positive if British higher)	4.90		3.96		4.52	
t value	8.53		7.22		11.28	
Significance of difference p<	.01		.01		.01	

Table 3.24: Personality differences between American college students and British undergraduates: Neuroticism Scale Questionnaire

	Females		Males		Females + Males	
	Mean	*SD*	*Mean*	*SD*	*Mean*	*SD*
British undergraduates N = 668 / N = 585 / N = 1256	43.01	6.96	37.60	7.92	40.48	7.89
American college students N = 393 / N = 675 / N = 1068	45.10	7.10	39.20	7.40	42.10	7.70
Difference in mean (positive if British higher)	−2.09		−1.60		−1.62	
t value	4.68		3.70		4.99	
Significance of difference p<	.01		.01		.01	

Table 3.25: Personality differences between American college and British university students: 16PF

	A	B	C	E	F	G	H	I	L	M	N	O	Q1	Q2	Q3	Q4
Females *A + B*	A**	B**	A**	NS	A**	A**	A**	NS	NS	B**	A**	B**	B**	B**	A**	NS
Females *C + D*	A**	B**	B**	B*	A**	A**	A**	B**	A**	B**	A**	A**	B**	B**	A**	A*
Males *A + B*	A**	B**	NS	A*	A**	A**	A**	B**	NS	B**	NS	NS	B**	B**	NS	A**
Males *C + D*	A*	B**	NS	NS	A**	A**	A**	B**	A**	B**	A**	A**	B**	B**	A**	A**

A: American college students significantly higher
B: British university students significantly higher

* p<.01
** p<.05

differences are the cause or the effect of academic specialization. But bearing in mind that they are of some considerable magnitude, as are some of the sex differences, we have thought it best to publish separate discipline as well as separate sex norms (Saville and Blinkhorn, 1976 (a), (b) and (c)).

The extent of the differences we report are clearly not without significance for the users of personality tests. Particularly where small groups are concerned, it may be of great importance to pay close attention to our findings. Although differences are small on certain factors, others, notably Factor I, seem to be particularly sensitive to group differences and neglect of this fact may affect experimental results when the test is used as a baseline measure.

The number of consistent differences we have found leads us to the view that the 16PF is likely to prove more descriptively useful than the EPI, despite the higher reliability of Eysenck's scales, even though it may be that fewer than 16 dimensions are needed to account for the differences. Notable also is the extent to which the 16PF differences seem to tie in well with popular prejudice.

The test user is therefore faced with the problem of handling a trade-off between rich descriptive complexity and the statistical problems involved in using a multiplicity of correlated scales. Careful note should also be taken of inter-form inconsistencies, where they occur.

It is clearly of the first importance to describe results not merely in terms of trait names but in terms also of the particular form of the 16PF used. Group differences are just one of the many facets of the validity of a test, and carry no guarantee that the named traits are indeed measured by the corresponding scales. A further major consideration is the reliability of each scale and this chapter must ultimately be considered in the light of the next.

Chapter 4

Reliability of the Cattell Scales

Introduction to reliability theory

Every measuring device is subject to some degree of error and inaccuracy, whether it be the simplest ruler or the most complicated of electronic instruments. The same applies to psychological tests and questionnaires: they do not measure with absolute and definitive precision; rather, there is an inherent margin of error which must be taken into account if a sound and reasonable judgement is to be made on the basis of obtained scores. This is the vital concept of scale reliability, the accuracy of measurement without prejudice to the dimension being measured. Precision of measurement is of necessity one of the principal aims of the scientist, and in the case of the psychometrician it is improved by maximizing the reliability of his scales.

Whereas in the case of a device designed to measure physical phenomena this accuracy is generally expressed in terms of a band of tolerance about the observed measurement, in psychometrics the reliability coefficient is the accepted index. This is a correlation coefficient which expresses the extent to which a particular scale agrees with itself in scores it yields for the same set of individuals. Essentially, two or more sets of scores are obtained for the same group of individuals, and correlation coefficients are calculated. These co-efficients are then taken as estimates of the reliability of the scale. The methods used for obtaining the different sets of scores vary — for a fuller exposition of the theory and practice of reliability estimation, the reader should consult a standard text on psychometrics such as Cronbach (1970), Guilford (1954), Nunally (1967) or, for the mathematically sophisticated, Lord and Novick (1968) — what follows is a brief and necessarily incomplete account of the possible techniques. Whichever technique is used, however, it remains the case that the coefficient obtained is an estimate of the reliability of the scale rather than any absolute value. That is to say, the use of different methods and different samples as a basis for estimating reliability will tend to result in differing estimates. For this reason it is advantageous to base such estimates on as large, as representative and as relevant a group as is reasonably possible.

Since there is an element of error inherent in all measurement, it is necessary to assess the relative importance of random fluctuations in a given set of measurements. Each technique for assessing reliability isolates different elements contributing to the scores and counts some as true measurement (true score variance) and others as contaminating, error factors (error variance).

Homogeneity, or internal consistency, is a reliability index widely used where tests of attainment and ability are concerned, and is especially convenient since only a single test administration is needed. In its purest form, it is based on item statistics, and counts as true score variance only that part of the variance of any item which is common to at least one other item. This is Cronbach's coefficient alpha. Commonly, however, it is estimated by approximate formulae or by arbitrarily splitting the items in a test into two or more subtests according to some convenient system, and taking the correlation corrected for test length as the reliability coefficient.

Test-retest reliability, on the other hand, is estimated by repeat administration of the same test. Irregular change in scores between the two administrations is treated as error. Cattell (1970) has distinguished between the 'dependability' coefficient where the retest session follows too soon for the subject themselves to change and the 'stability' coefficient, where two months or more may elapse between the two administrations of the test.

Stability is a very important concept in trait psychology: in the calculation of stability coefficients both relative shifts in score due to real changes in the individual and shifts attributable to random measurement error are treated as error variance. Clearly the researcher will want to be able to distinguish between these two sources of 'error' so as to be able to evaluate real changes in the individual. Attempts have been made to separate traits which are relatively stable from shorter-term influences which are more bound to particular situations and change in strength over a short period. For example, the State-Trait Anxiety Inventory (Spielberger *et al.*, 1970) seeks to isolate those aspects of anxiety which are situationally dependent (state) from those which are a more stable feature of the make-up of the individual (trait). From the point of view of reliability theory, it is important to recognize that the length of time which elapses between test and retest may be an important determinant of the size of the test-retest coefficient.

The third commonly used index of reliability is the alternate form coefficient, otherwise known as the equivalence or parallel forms coefficient. The different names all represent — from different theoretical standpoints — the correlation of scores on one form of a test with scores on another form designed to measure the same characteristics. That is to say, the alternate form coefficient is a measure of the extent to which two distinct forms which are designed to measure the same thing actually do so.

All three methods of estimating reliability, and others besides, have been used from time to time with respect to the 16PF. In particular, the usefulness of the homogeneity coefficient for Cattell's oblique factors, as measured by short scales, has been a matter of some debate. Levonian (1961) amongst others has criticized the 16PF scales for having demonstrably low internal consistency. In reply, Cattell has claimed that this is a positive advantage where items have been chosen to represent a factor in a short scale. Items having high correlations with the factor, but low intercorrelations amongst themselves, will tend to have the highest multiple correlation with the factor, which is important if the scale is to be valid, i.e. measure what it is designed to measure, as well as reliable. A scale made up of such items will tend to have low homogeneity (Cattell, 1974).

We have hinted above that there may arise difficulties in interpreting the significance of test-retest coefficients, but of the importance and interpretation of alternate form reliability coefficients there can be no doubt. Alternate form reliability is indubitably highly relevant to personality questionnaires and their construction, and the experimental design adopted for this survey, with counterbalanced administration order, makes it ideal for the purpose of investigating reliability by this method. An alternate form coefficient is an estimate of the extent to which two scales measure the same underlying variable. One may think of it, as Cattell has suggested, as the coefficient of 'structured homogeneity'.

As well as providing an estimate of reliability, the alternate form coefficient tells us how successful the scale constructor has been in pinning down the construct he set out to measure in terms of actual scale items. Generally, the availability of alternate forms of tests mirrors the difficulty of measuring a particular construct: as the complexity and theoretical sophistication of the construct increases, so alternate forms become more difficult to construct and indeed, rarer. The Cattell and Eysenck inventories stand almost alone amongst established personality questionnaires in having alternate forms.

Reliability of the 16PF first and second order factors

The construction of alternate forms for attainment tests is a relatively straightforward procedure: not only will the alternate forms be equivalent in the sense of having a high intercorrelation, but they will also, if properly constructed, have the same raw score means and standard deviations in the reference population. With increasing complexity in the behaviour being tapped, the parameters relevant to item selection become less obvious and the availability of equivalent items is reduced. The actual trait or ability to be measured will tend to be less clear-cut, and some sacrifices may have to be made with respect to the more stringent requirements of parallel-form theory. Thus, the scales measuring the same factors in alternate forms of the 16PF do not in general give identical raw score means and standard deviations, although this is in part compensated for by the adoption of the N-sten standard score system.

Nonetheless, given that alternate forms are published and used, high alternate form correlation is an indispensible requirement. The scales on each form bear the same factor name, and the user has the right to expect that they measure essentially the same traits. The profile sheets for the 16PF are identical for different forms: there is no suggestion that, say, Factor N, Form A is a different factor from Factor N, Form B. We must expect this identity of printing to be supported by an underlying identity of factor measurement. Of course, using more than one form and consolidating scores on the different forms will reduce the error inherent in measurement (total scale length is a most important determinant of reliability) but if two purportedly equivalent scales correlate hardly at all, the resulting composite may be like nothing so much as a mixture of oil and water.

Cattell provides the alternate form reliability coefficients for the first order factors for the 16PF only. In the tables which follow we also present the alternate form reliabilities of the second order factors and derived criteria: these could be mathematically derived from the reliabilities, first order factor intercorrelations and standard deviations, but in fact we have calculated them directly from the data.

Table 4.1 gives the alternate form reliability coefficients for the first order factors of the 16PF Form A with B and Form C with D. The first order results are in general higher than those reported by Cattell, Eber and Tatsuoka (1970). Nevertheless, the reliability coefficients are rather lower than we have come to expect in psychological measurement. Only Factors F, H and possibly Q4 in Forms A and B are of roughly the same order of magnitude as one finds with cognitive tests. Against this of course one must bear in mind that ability tests are typically longer and that measurement in the affective domain is generally less precise than in the cognitive.

Most of the Form A with B reliabilities range from .4 to .7 and the majority of coefficients in the Form C with D study from .3 to .5;

Table 4.1: Alternate form reliabilities of the 16PF first order factors

	A	B	C	E	F	G	H	I	L	M	N	O	Q1	Q2	Q3	Q4
Form A with B																
Females N = 599	65	37	51	57	71	57	81	47	34	28	29	59	51	47	56	68
Males N = 549	61	35	56	55	71	57	78	58	35	40	23	66	42	50	58	68
Both sexes N = 1148	64	36	54	59	70	56	80	60	36	23	26	65	47	48	58	70
Form C with D																
Females N = 609	53	18	48	41	44	49	65	40	29	32	15	47	40	44	42	51
Males N = 549	54	32	54	49	46	52	60	49	31	27	13	59	38	30	43	53
Both sexes N = 1158	53	26	51	46	45	51	52	50	30	30	14	55	39	38	42	51

Decimal points have been omitted from this table.
All correlations are positive.

clearly the greater number of items in the A and B Forms has a bearing here. Also worthy of note is the relatively close correspondence between the findings on the two sets of forms in that higher reliabilities are generally to be found for example on Factors A, H, O and Q4, whilst the "problem" Factors L, M and N show low coefficients across both the studies.

The reliability of Factor B on both pairs of forms is rather lower than most other factors: this may be the result of shorter scale length (10 items only) but is more probably due to the effects of restriction in the range of obtained scores. Undergraduates are, after all, selected largely on grounds of academic ability, which is reflected in high scores on Factor B: restriction of range of scores tends to depress the reliability coefficient. The restriction in range phenomenon would not seem to apply however to the other 16PF factors because in general the undergraduate samples show not less but greater variability than British adults, for example (see Table 3.5).

Table 4.2 presents alternate form reliability coefficients for the second order factors and principal derived criterion scales of the 16PF. Since many more items contribute to each second order factor than to each first order factor, it is to be expected that these scales should have higher reliabilities. In the case of Exvia and Anxiety in Forms A and B, the coefficients are about as high as one could reasonably expect (.81 to .84) and their counterparts in Forms C and D appear to be not unsatisfactory in this regard (.69 to .77). Moreover, the eighth second order factor, Super-Ego Strength, also seems relatively sound in terms of reliability. On the other hand, one could wish for much improved reliability for the other second order factors, and in particular for Discreetness; however, it is only the first four of the second order factors which Cattell claims are truly well established. This should of course be borne in mind when interpreting scores. In particular, the second order intelligence factor, composed largely of the first order Factor B, gains nothing in reliability from the contributions made by other first order factors — indeed, it may even lose a little.

Reliability of the NSQ and IAS

The IPAT Anxiety Scale and Neuroticism Scale Questionnaire do not have alternate forms, but estimates of their reliabilities can be derived nonetheless from their relationship with the second order factors of the 16PF. The IPAT Anxiety Scale is designed to measure the second order Anxiety factor of the 16PF, and so a direct estimate of its reliability may be obtained by calculating its correlations with the 16PF Forms C and D Anxiety factor. These correlations are presented in Table 4.3 (The reader will remember that this scale was only used with Forms C / D of the 16PF).

Table 4.2: Alternate form reliabilities of the 16PF second order factors and derived criteria

	Second order factors								Derived criteria			
	Exvia	Anxiety	Corter-tia	Indepen-dence	Discreet-tness	Prodigal subject-ivity	Intelli-gence	Super-ego str-engtb	Neurot-icism	Leader-ship	Creati-vity	School achieve-ment
	QI	QII	QIII	QIV	QV	QVI	QVII	QVIII				
Form A with B												
Females N = 599	83	81	56	68	46	44	35	71	73	77	59	50
Males N = 549	84	84	60	67	29	55	34	69	78	82	62	54
Total (N = 1148)	84	82	58	67	38	52	35	70	76	80	60	51
Form C with D												
Females N = 609	72	76	50	58	20	35	19	60	64	71	52	36
Males N = 549	69	77	53	58	16	50	29	61	68	70	52	44
Total N = 1158	71	74	56	58	18	45	25	60	66	70	52	40

Decimal points have been omitted from this table.
All correlations are positive

Table 4.3: Correlations of the IPAT Anxiety Scale (IAS) with the 16PF second order Anxiety factor

	Form C Anxiety	Form D Anxiety	Ford C + D Anxiety
Females	.73	.71	.77
Males	.76	.77	.81
Total	.73	.71	.78

Things are not quite so straightforward with regard to the NSQ. As compared with the Neuroticism derived criterion, the NSQ total score was designed to have 50 per cent less Anxiety component. The reasons for this are discussed in the manual to the NSQ, and are essentially related to the clinical application of the instrument and the advantages to be gained from exaggerating the contribution of the non-anxiety components for diagnostic purposes. Nonetheless, the relevant scale for comparison is the Neuroticism derived criterion in the 16PF — the two scales do after all bear the same name — and these correlations are given in Table 4.4.

Table 4.4: Correlations of the Neuroticism Scale Questionnaire (NSQ) with the 16PF Neuroticism derived criterion

	Form C Neuroticism	Form D Neuroticism	Form C + D Neuroticism
Females	.62	.55	.58
Males	.60	.64	.69
Total	.55	.55	.61

It will be observed that the correlations between the IAS and NSQ and their corresponding 16PF scales are closely comparable to the reliability of the 16PF scales in question. We may, therefore, take it that the reliability of the IAS and NSQ total scores are reasonably estimated by these correlations. The scores on the constitutive first order factors in the IAS and NSQ are not here examined in terms of reliability on account of their brevity.

Standard errors of measurement

What do these reliability coefficients mean in practice? One way of interpreting them is in terms of the Standard Error of Measurement (SE_M). This statistic describes the band of error around test scores — and is the estimated standard deviation of scores which would be obtained if an individual were given a large number of parallel tests. The SE_M gives us some idea of the extent of discrepancies caused by errors of measurement and is estimated by the formula:

$$SE_M = SD_t \sqrt{(1-r_t)}$$

Where SE_M = standard error of measurement.

SD_t = standard deviation of obtained scores

r_t = reliability coefficient

The SE_M statistic is important because it enables us to set up confidence zones for obtained scores. A test or questionnaire with a SE_M equal to 1.5 units for example, indicates that in about two out of three cases the observed scores will lie within 1.5 units of the true scores.

Strictly speaking, the confidence limits described by use of the SE_M refer not to the zone in which the true score is likely to lie: rather, they describe the zone around the true score in which the observed score is likely to lie. Whilst this distinction is important from the point of view of psychometric theory, for practical purposes, so long as no further statistical arguments are based on the confidence level, this point is unimportant. The user can never know what the true score actually is, merely how good an estimate he has in the form of an observed score.

In Tables 4.5 and 4.6 the Standard Errors of Measurement have been calculated in n-sten units on the basis of the total sexes reliability coefficients reported above. In the case of Form A+B and Form C+D, the reliabilities have been corrected by the Spearman-Brown formula before the Standard Errors of Measurement of the factors were calculated.

The Spearman-Brown Formula:

$$r_t = \frac{2r_{ab}}{1+r_{ab}}$$

Where r_{ab} = correlation of Forms A and B for a given factor
r_t = reliability corrected for two form length.

Table 4.5: Standard errors of measurement in π-sten units of the 16PF first order factors

	A	B	C	E	F	G	H	I	L	M	N	O	Q1	Q2	Q3	Q4
Form A / B	1.20	1.60	1.36	1.28	1.10	1.33	.89	1.27	1.60	1.76	1.72	1.18	1.46	1.44	1.30	1.10
Forms A+B*	.94	1.37	1.09	1.02	.84	1.06	.67	1.00	1.37	1.58	1.53	.92	1.20	1.19	1.03	.84
Form C / D	1.37	1.72	1.40	1.47	1.48	1.40	1.23	1.41	1.67	1.67	1.86	1.34	1.56	1.57	1.52	1.40
Forms C+D*	1.11	1.53	1.14	1.22	1.23	1.14	.97	1.16	1.47	1.47	1.74	1.08	1.33	1.34	1.28	1.14

* Corrected to two form length by the Spearman-Brown formula.

Table 4.6: Standard errors of measurement in n-sten units of the 16PF second order factors and derived criteria

| | Second order factors | | | | | | | | Derived criteria | | | |
	Exvia QI	Anxiety QII	Cortertia QIII	Independence QIV	Discreetness QV	Prodigal subjectivity QVI	Intelligence QVII	Superego strengtb QVIII	Neuroticism	Leadersbip	Creativity	School achievement
Form A / B	.80	.80	1.27	1.15	1.69	1.34	1.63	1.11	.94	.85	1.23	1.36
Forms A+B*	.59	.63	1.03	.89	1.34	1.12	1.39	.84	.74	.67	1.00	1.14
Form C / D	1.08	1.02	1.33	1.30	1.81	1.48	1.73	1.27	1.17	1.10	1.39	1.55
Forms C+D*	.82	.77	1.06	1.03	1.67	1.23	1.55	1.00	.91	.84	1.12	1.31

* Corrected to two form length by the Spearman-Brown formula.

If the SE_M is large, interpretation of scores can only be made with less certainty than is justified when the SE_M is small. In most applied work a margin of two SE_M's is usually allowed around obtained test scores; this corresponds to a 95 per cent confidence zone. Thus, from Table 4.5 the odds are 19 to 1 that on Factor I for Forms A+B the observed score will be within two stens of the true score. It is important to realize that because high scores tend to be biased upward and low scores downward, confidence zones are not symmetrical about the obtained score. Nevertheless, if we arbitrarily take an observed sten score of 5.5 it is possible to plot two SE_M's about this value without having to correct for bias. Diagrams 4.1 and 4.2 illustrate the 95% confidence zones around such a score for the first and second order factors for the 16PF.

The diagrams present a visual representation of the range in standard errors of measurement in the form of confidence bands about the mean score of the n-sten distribution: only the range for Forms C or D and Forms A+B are given: other values lie in between these two extremes. If three or more forms are used, then the SE_M will be correspondingly reduced, but as we do not have data based on the administration of three or four forms together, we have preferred not to estimate these values.

The important lesson of diagrams 4.1 and 4.2 is that most particularly where the scores of a single individual are concerned, too great a burden of interpretation should not be placed on relatively small differences in scores between scales. For instance, in the worst case we can envisage amongst first order factors *viz.* Factor N on either Form C or Form D used alone, the 95 per cent confidence limits about the mean of 5.5 are at the 2nd and 9th stens. On the other hand, the best case is Factor H on Forms A and B used together, where the limits are at the 4th and 7th stens. The moral of these figures quite clearly is that a danger exists of reading into the configuration of a profile cconsiderably more precision than the scales themselves are capable of providing. Where decisions may be made about the fortunes of individual people based on comparatively minor differences in scores, this possibility is most disturbing. Indeed many authors, for example Cronbach (1970) and Nunally (1967) advise that reliability of the order of .9 is the minimum acceptable if decisions about individuals are to be made on the basis of test scores. Such reliability expressed in sten score SE_M units is of the order of .6. The only scales on the 16PF which show such precision are Factor H amongst the first order factors, and that only when Forms A and B are administered together, and the second orders Exvia and Anxiety, and the derived criterion for Leadership, again for Forms A and B administered together.

Taking another approach, one might ask how long would the scales

Figure 4.1: The 95 per cent confidence zones about A Sten score of 5.5 for the 16PF First Order Factors

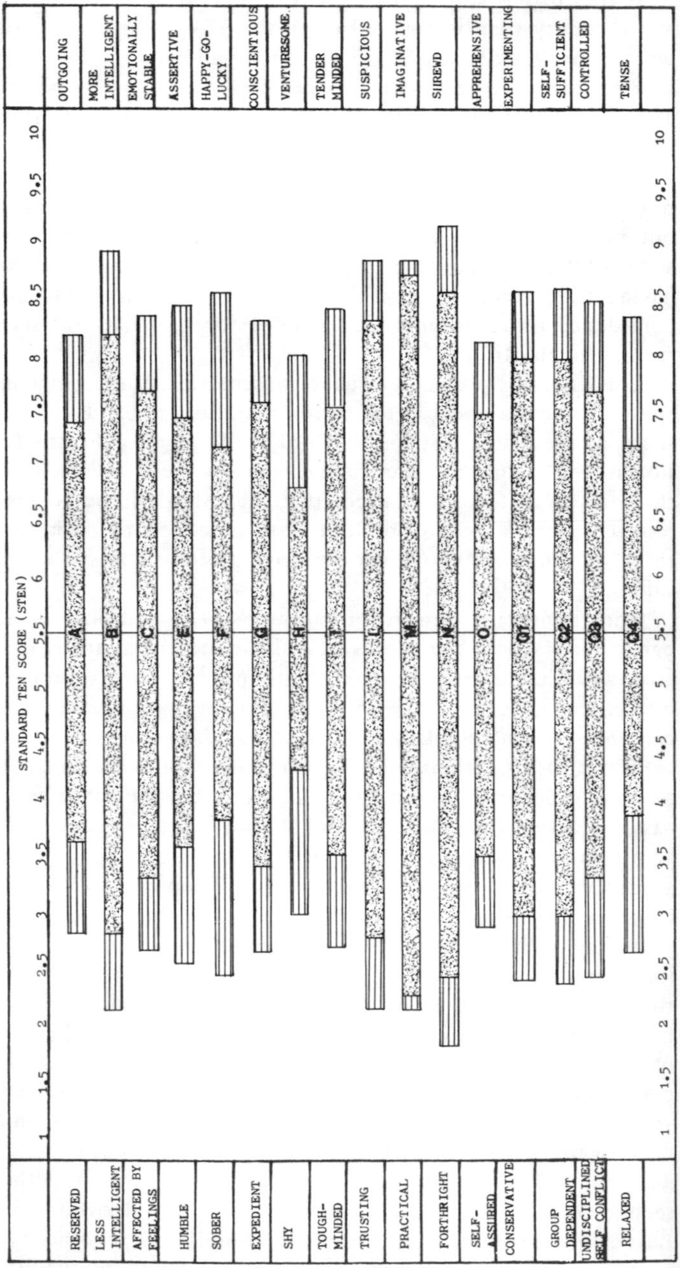

Figure 4.2: The 95 per cent confidence zones about A Sten scores of 5.5 for the 16PF Second Order Factors

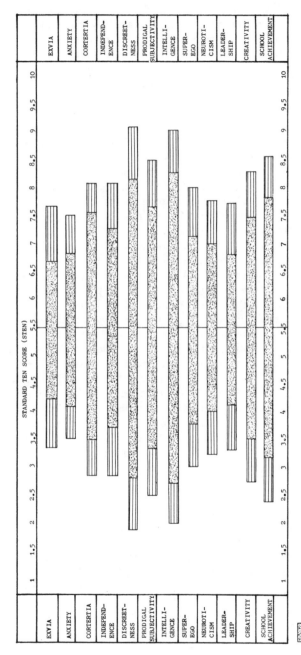

95% CONFIDENCE ZONE 16PF FORMS A + B

95% CONFIDENCE ZONE 16PF FORMS C or D

have to be were they all to reach a reliability of .9? This can be estimated by rearranging the Spearman-Brown formula to solve for n and we find that to achieve alternate-form reliability of .9 for all the scales in the 16PF, it would be necessary to increase the length of the questionnaire by a factor of 10 in the case of Form A or B. Of course, much of this increase in length would have to be devoted to the least reliable scales and it is questionable whether sufficient items could ever be found to achieve this end. For example, Factor N alone would require approximately 395 items, which would need about one and a half hours testing time before the recommended reliability for individual interpretation was obtained!

However, this represents a hard line in reliability theory. In more recent times it has been realized that although an author will take great care to ensure that his measurement is of high precision, scales with reliabilities as low as .5 may in fact be potentially useful devices particularly where testing time is limited and measures of several variables are needed (the 'fidelity-bandwidth' dilemma).

We shall see in Chapter 6, for example, that despite the apparent unreliability of the 16PF Factor B (Intelligence), it is an efficient discriminator between students and general population young adults.

These issues, though of interest, need not concern us unduly here, for scale reliability must mainly be judged on the particular use to which a test is being put. Nevertheless, by the commonly accepted standards of reliability the first order scales of the 16PF do not fare well, at least in this undergraduate population. However, this may largely be due to the small number of items contributing to each scale although there is little defence to be made for, say Factors L, M and N. As Cattell has often pointed out, one cannot over-emphasize the need to use more than a single form if reliable measurement is to be achieved, most particularly when scores are to be interpreted on an individual basis. Further, if alternate forms of the 16PF are to be used to detect change due to some experimental treatment without the safeguard of a control group, close attention should be paid to these reliability estimates.

As a further point, it is a sobering thought that if we were to take a regression approach and use these alternate form correlations as a means of estimating a sten of an individual on one form of the 16PF, given the score on the other, the error in prediction (known as the Standard Error of Estimate) is even larger than the SE_M figures given in Tables 4.5 & 4.6. (The Standard Error of Estimate is in fact $\sqrt{1+r}$ as large again as the Standard Error of Measurement.) Finally, Table 4.7 summarizes the results discussed in this chapter in tabular form.

Table 4.7: Summary table of 16PF reliabilities

		Form combination			
		A + B	C + D	A / B	C / D
Confidence zone outer limits 4th–7th stens SE_M = .75 + below r = .86 +	1st Orders	H,			
	2nd orders	QI, QII,			
	Derived criteria				
Confidence zone outer limits 3rd–8th stens SE_M = .76 −1.25 r = .61 − .85	1st Orders	A,C,E,F,G, I,O,Q1,Q2, Q3,Q4,	A,C,E,F,C, H,I,O,Q4,	A,F,H,O,Q4,	H,
	2nd Orders	QIII,QIV, QVI,QVIII,	QI,QH,QIII, QIV,QVI, QVIII,	QI,QII,QIV, QVIII,	QI,QII,
	Derived criteria	Neur, Lead, Creat, Sch. Ach.	Neur, Lead Creat.	Neur, Lead Creat.	Neur, Lead
Confidence zone outer limits 2.5–8.5 stens SE_M = 1.26 − 1.50 r = .44 − .60	1st Orders	B,L,	L,M, Q1,Q2,Q3,	C,E,G,I, Q1,Q2,Q3,	A,C,E,F,G,I O,Q4
	2nd Orders	QV,QVII,		QIII, QVI,	QIII,QIV QVI,QVIII,
	Derived criteria		Sch.Ach,	Sch.Ach,	Creat,
Confidence zone outer limits 2nd–9th stens SE_M = 1.51 + r = .43 + below	1st Orders	M,N,	B,N,	B,L,M,N,	B,L,M,N, Q1,Q2,Q3,
	2nd Orders		QV,QVII	QV,QVII,	QV,QVII
	Derived criteria				Sch.Ach.

Intercorrelations between the 16PF factors

Tables 4.9 to 4.14 give the intercorrelations of the first and second order factors of the 16PF for Forms A, B, A+B, C, D and C+D. Decimal points have been omitted from the tables and correlations are positive unless otherwise indicated. The fact that there are significant correlations between the factor scales comes as no surprise, of course, since Cattell deliberately aimed to produce oblique rather than orthogonal factors, that is to say, factors which are themselves intercorrelated.

In the separate matrices for male and female students, each of which contains 120 correlations, about 75 per cent of the correlations are significant at the .05 level and approximately half are significant at the .01 level or beyond.

In the light of the concepts of convergent and discriminant validity however, it is in the comparison of these coefficients with the alternate form reliability coefficients that these tables become most significant (Campbell and Fiske, 1959). From the point of view of the user of personality questionnaires whose interest in basic research in personality extends only so far as the availability of useful measuring instruments, this comparison is vital. Where a scale correlates more highly with a scale bearing a different name than it does with its own alternate form, or when these correlations are so close that sampling error might be held to account for the discrepancy, the adequacy of the scale as a measure of a well-defined factor is open to doubt. This question, we must emphasize, is to do with the properties of questionnaire scales, not with the ultimate underlying structure of personality, whatever that may be. When, as with Factors C, O and Q4 the intercorrelations and alternate form reliability coefficients are all of very similar values, it is hard to see any justification for asserting their separate identity.

To illustrate the point more clearly, let us examine the intercorrelations between Factors C, O and Q4 on Forms A and B for both sexes combined (N = 1148). (This pattern of intercorrelation is discernable with Factors C, O and Q4 for all forms of the 16PF). The correlation coefficients in rectangles are the alternate form reliabilities. Factor C (Emotional Stability), Factor O (Guilt Proneness) and Factor Q4 (Tension) as three of the main contributors to Cattell's second order of Anxiety, are in practice difficult to distinguish as separate entities. Indeed we can have the situation where Emotional Stability (C) would appear better measured by Guilt Proneness (O) and Tension (Q4) than by itself! There is a similar trend for reliabilities to be of the same order as scale intercorrelations with the Exvia / Invia constellation of Assertiveness (E), Happy-go-luckiness (F) and Social Boldness (H) (See Tables 4.8 to 4.13).

Table 4.8: Intercorrelation of Factors C, O and Q4 for both sexes

		Form A			Form B		
		C	O	Q4	C	O	Q4
Form A	C		−56	−62	54	−61	−57
	O			64	−56	65	64
	Q4				−58	66	70
Form B	C					−61	−57
	O						60
	Q4						

The intercorrelation matrices of the second order factors are contained in Tables 4.15 to 4.18. The correlations for males are given above and the values for females below the main diagonal in each table. These second orders have been calculated by way of American stens and the separate weights for the sexes provided by Cattell (1970).

It can be seen that Cattell's two main second order factors of Exvia and Anxiety are not orthogonal but are to some extent negatively correlated. The Prodigal Subjectivity second order factor which is defined by Cattell (1973) as 'an imaginative interest in idealistic change in relation to subjective goals as opposed to a practical acceptance of existing realities', shows clear sex differences in its relationship with the other second order factors. This is no doubt in part due to the very different weights for the two sexes, for example, Factor L receives a high positive weight for females but a high negative weight for males.

Another second order factor of some interest is Tough Poise, or 'Cortertia' which is Cattell's abbreviation for cortical alertness. The scale shows relatively high positive correlations with Exvia in females and low positive in male groups. As a matter of interest, this seems to be the direct opposite of Eysenck's thinking where it is the introvert who has lower cortical arousal thresholds.

With regard to the second of the four derived criteria measures, Leadership shows a high positive correlation with Exvia and a high negative correlation with Anxiety in all the matrices. In fact the

Table 4.9: 16PF first order factors intercorrelations: Form A

Female N = 599

Factor	A	B	C	E	F	G	H	I	L	M	N	O	Q1	Q2	Q3	Q4
A		00	07	04	29	11	32	16	06	05	10	-14	-05	-32	03	-12
B	-05		-01	-05	-13	03	-07	04	-03	04	-04	-09	05	00	06	-07
C	14	-02		-01	17	-03	27	-08	-35	11	-09	-55	04	-16	27	-63
E	11	-07	14		48	-27	55	-05	41	11	-36	-08	35	-10	-27	08
F	27	-11	19	48		-28	59	03	22	08	-27	-12	22	-33	-28	-05
G	18	-05	08	-15	-12		-06	-06	-17	-20	27	-02	-25	01	51	-07
H	40	-10	37	56	60	08		-04	12	08	-24	-32	20	-31	-01	-23
I	09	-13	-22	-06	-05	-16	02		04	26	10	06	-03	13	-13	06
L	09	-14	-24	35	26	-10	14	04		-01	-16	29	24	09	-33	43
M	09	-13	12	19	10	-14	19	23	-03		-11	-14	18	01	-16	-13
N	-06	04	-15	-36	-41	06	-34	06	-14	-11		08	-24	09	23	02
O	-15	01	-58	-24	-18	-16	-43	13	17	-21	19		-08	16	-28	61
Q1	-02	-01	06	38	24	-23	21	-05	24	17	-16	-16		-01	-22	02
Q2	-37	03	-03	-12	-37	-13	-32	-02	-06	01	14	04	00		-01	17
Q3	09	-04	29	-16	-10	55	12	-17	-17	-07	04	-36	-10	00		-38
Q4	-09	-01	-63	-07	-09	-16	-33	14	30	-15	12	62	-06	00	-04	

Male N = 549

Table 4.10: 16PF first order factors intercorrelations: Form B

Female N = 599 (upper triangle) / Male N = 549 (lower triangle)

Factor	A	B	C	E	F	G	H	I	L	M	N	O	Q1	Q2	Q3	Q4
A		04	18	07	28	02	37	10	-14	-08	06	-20	12	-38	00	-03
B	-01		09	-02	-07	05	04	01	-04	-05	07	-04	03	02	10	-05
C	11	02		-10	04	10	30	-03	-34	-12	22	-58	-09	-24	41	-56
E	18	-03	08		27	-25	33	-18	23	37	-28	-13	37	18	-07	13
F	35	-08	10	38		-31	48	-17	-03	09	-23	-22	15	-34	-20	15
G	12	-01	10	-17	-22		-11	07	01	-20	28	-02	-23	-04	39	-21
H	34	-05	40	40	55	06		-07	-12	14	-01	-50	14	-36	23	-20
I	13	07	-12	11	-12	14	-11		-09	18	04	09	-06	-06	-09	00
L	02	-05	-27	27	12	-08	-04	-13		-06	-15	27	12	27.	-08	35
M	03	02	-01	29	11	-07	14	26	-07		-27	-04	39	10	-23	05
N	-04	-04	19	-31	-32	19	-10	-01	19	-26		-09	-16	-04	28	-29
O	-16	05	-62	-22	-24	-05	-56	23	18	-03	-11		-06	22	-34	55
Q1	11	06	-06	30	13	-12	10	00	16	36	-21	-06		01	-10	13
Q2	-32	02	-23	-07	-37	-11	-43	06	15	11	04	19	04		-04	11
Q3	-01	00	37	07	-12	36	23	-08	-07	-06	21	-42	-07	-08		-45
Q4	-02	00	-57	-07	09	-19	-31	17	27	04	-26	60	05	11	-46	

Table 4.11: 16PF first order factors intercorrelations: Form A+B

Female N = 599 (above diagonal) — Male N = 549 (below diagonal)

Factor	A	B	C	E	F	G	H	I	L	M	N	O	Q1	Q2	Q3	Q4
A		04	17	07	35	06	40	16	-09	-03	09	-21	04	-46	03	10
B	06		05	-05	-13	07	-01	03	-03	00	03	-09	08	00	11	-10
C	16	01		04	13	08	34	-11	-48	03	08	-70	-03	-25	43	-71
E	19	-08	14		46	-33	51	-15	40	36	-47	-14	47	00	-21	14
F	37	14	17	52		-35	60	-09	14	13	-32	-19	23	-42	-28	05
G	16	-04	14	57	64		-10	00	-10	-29	37	-01	-32	-03	56	-17
H	44	-10	45	-10	-11	07		-07	-01	14	-18	-47	20	-41	08	-25
I	15	13	-24	37	24	-01	-09		-06	28	09	10	-07	04	-11	05
L	06	10	-35	32	11	-12	05	-06		02	-22	37	25	22	-29	55
M	05	03	06	-47	-44	-16	21	33	-05		02	-11	39	05	-25	-05
N	-08	04	02	-29	-24	19	-32	02	-23	-15		-33	-30	03	33	-17
O	-20	02	-75	44	24	-13	-55	24	22	35	07		-05	23	-40	70
Q1	07	08	00	-11	-47	-25	21	-05	30	06	-23	-14		02	-20	09
Q2	-44	-02	-16	-05	-14	-16	-44	05	04	-12	15	15	02		-04	17
Q3	06	00	-05	-07	-01	59	22	-16	-17	-09	21	-49	-11	-05		04
Q4	-08		-07			-21	-36	18	39		-08	72	-01	08	-53	

Table 4.12: 16PF first order factors intercorrelations: Form C

Upper right triangle: Female N = 609; Lower left triangle: Male N = 549

Factor	A	B	C	E	F	G	H	I	L	M	N	O	Q1	Q2	Q3	Q4
A		-03	21	-01	27	02	34	16	-03	04	-10	-11	03	-45	05	-05
B	-08		-01	-06	-06	03	-06	-04	-02	00	03	05	-01	-02	00	05
C	21	-08		-09	18	08	27	02	-22	-08	-11	-34	01	-19	27	-37
E	12	-06	03		26	-15	22	-02	23	02	-05	-12	15	05	-12	15
F	30	-03	09	35		-13	54	03	06	-02	-08	-19	07	-28	-05	01
G	-02	02	03	-18	-26		-01	-11	-06	-07	09	10	-14	-09	32	-06
H	30	-09	31	28	44	-12		05	05	03	-19	-31	14	-26	-01	-06
I	10	02	-07	-09	-04	-11	-03		02	28	01	01	22	-03	-14	12
L	-08	-11	-15	27	19	-05	14	-03		09	10	10	14	09	-12	27
M	00	00	-12	-04	-07	-05	-05	41	04		-02	00	39	07	-12	10
N	-09	06	-23	-09	-18	06	-29	03	03	10		28	-08	06	12	13
O	-12	03	-45	-12	-13	07	-35	01	16	08	33		-15	05	-13	39
Q1	12	01	05	17	09	-16	12	34	08	30	-05	-06		07	-18	02
Q2	-37	03	-19	-06	-23	03	-29	08	11	11	08	06	06		-12	10
Q3	07	00	27	-12	-19	34	03	-14	-14	-10	03	-17	-09	-12		-30
Q4	-03	01	-43	12	05	-05	-10	04	28	08	21	57	04	11	-31	

Table 4.13: 16PF first order factors intercorrelations: Form D

Female N = 609 (above diagonal)   Male N = 549 (below diagonal)

Factor	A	B	C	E	F	G	H	I	L	M	N	O	Q1	Q2	Q3	Q4
A		00	11	01	27	00	40	23	-04	08	-10	-01	07	-22	-04	00
B	00		01	-08	04	-06	-02	03	02	05	00	-05	00	-10	01	00
C	06	01		-08	24	01	27	05	-21	-05	-23	-42	-01	-19	30	-40
E	02	-03	-06		04	-22	25	-23	24	05	08	-08	28	07	-21	-05
F	28	01	13	16		-05	31	-11	00	-21	-16	-18	02	-38	07	-07
G	-01	03	05	-31	-14		-04	08	-11	-07	00	14	-33	-11	34	01
H	41	-06	26	24	26	-06		02	-02	08	-11	-23	22	-10	12	-32
I	29	-01	02	-25	-25	25	10		-07	22	-07	05	-02	09	03	-02
L	-02	-04	-21	18	00	-02	01	-14		02	12	13	10	08	-21	18
M	07	-03	-01	03	-14	-08	07	27	-04		02	07	20	23	-07	-03
N	-04	06	-18	04	-12	01	-13	-07	13	00		12	-07	04	-15	24
O	-01	-03	-55	-10	-18	13	-23	12	16	04	07		-05	13	-22	40
Q1	08	-07	00	31	17	-31	25	-07	12	14	-13	-07		11	-16	-07
Q2	-11	02	00	-05	-39	05	00	28	-05	25	-07	13	01		11	-16
Q3	-09	07	31	-16	-07	35	01	04	-11	-04	-16	-21	-11	01		-19
Q4	-03	02	-50	-07	-04	-04	-33	-01	22	-04	21	48	-11	-02	-33	

Table 4.14: 16PF first order factors intercorrelations: Form C+D

Female N = 609 (upper triangle) / Male N = 549 (lower triangle)

Factor	A	B	C	E	F	G	H	I	L	M	N	O	Q1	Q2	Q3	Q4
A		00	21	02	42	-01	46	26	-03	05	-12	-10	10	-47	03	-04
B	-07		-03	-07	01	-02	-05	-02	00	01	02	01	-03	-11	04	02
C	17	-04		-09	29	07	35	05	-30	-10	-28	-55	-01	-24	39	-55
E	42	-06	-01		21	-25	31	-20	34	03	00	-14	27	10	-24	05
F	10	-02	16	33		-11	54	-08	00	-15	-16	-22	06	-44	00	-07
G	-05	05	04	-32	-28		-04	-02	-10	-12	11	16	-34	-13	47	-05
H	46	-09	36	32	46	-13		07	05	07	-22	-36	26	-24	08	-24
I	26	00	-03	-24	-14	00	05		-05	39	-04	05	13	03	-08	04
L	-03	-08	-27	32	10	-07	08	-12		05	19	21	16	15	-26	32
M	08	00	-10	-04	-13	-11	04	49	-02		-04	07	43	24	-11	02
N	-04	08	-34	-04	-20	08	-31	00	19	03		30	-17	09	-01	28
O	-08	00	-65	-12	-15	12	-35	08	27	08	30		-11	08	-22	59
Q1	17	-07	05	29	16	-30	27	20	15	32	-19	-06		15	-23	-02
Q2	-36	04	-15	-06	-42	02	-21	21	10	31	04	11	12		-20	09
Q3	-01	07	37	-19	-19	48	03	-09	-16	-09	-06	-23	-11	-07		-38
Q4	-05	01	-62	04	-02	-06	-27	01	33	05	32	68	-04	06	-42	

Table 4.15: 16PF second order factors and derived criteria intercorrelations: Form A

Females N = 599 (upper triangle) · Male N = 549 (lower triangle)

	Exvia	Anxiety	Cortertia	Independence	Discreetness	Prodigal subjectivity	Intelligence	Super ego strength	Neuroticism	Leadership	Creativity	School Achievement
Exvia		-17	62	37	-44	42	-05	-22	-48	51	45	-34
Anxiety	-27		-04	-18	14	23	-03	-06	86	-75	02	-32
Cortertia	20	-20		43	-40	42	-16	-20	-34	40	-11	-34
Independence	53	-41	39		-60	35	07	-56	-32	03	49	01
Discreetness	-53	15	-40	-46		-05	-03	42	31	-07	-24	16
Prodigal Subjectivity	-09	03	00	12	-12		-10	-19	15	-02	16	-15
Intelligence	-14	-01	00	-03	02	22		03	-04	08	38	42
Super ego strength	-07	-16	-34	-34	21	-37	-05		10	38	-13	59
Neuroticism	-62	82	-44	-58	37	24	-05	-05		-80	22	-09
Leadership	64	-75	19	38	-24	-35	-04	46	-86		-29	28
Creativity	-35	-04	13	39	-10	62	41	-22	20	-27		43
School Achievement	17	-49	-11	21	-01	14	47	50	-24	36	45	

Table 4.16: 16PF second order factors and derived criteria intercorrelations: Form B

Females N = 599

Male N = 549

	Exvia	Anxiety	Cortertia	Independence	Discreetness	Prodigal subjectivity	Intelligence	Super ego strength	Neuroticism	Leadership	Creativity	School achievement
Exvia		−21	45	24	−34	24	00	−22	−52	51	−52	−30
Anxiety	−30		−17	−13	−09	12	−05	−17	80	−77	06	−32
Cortertia	20	−15		35	−28	10	−09	−09	−47	46	−12	−06
Independence	42	−30	35		−58	20	04	−44	−25	−06	54	32
Discreetness	−38	−18	−35	−41		03	05	46	11	16	−23	03
Prodigal subjectivity	−09	11	−09	07	−21		−07	−02	24	−03	24	03
Intelligence	−09	01	03	01	−06	11		08	−09	18	31	41
Super ego strength	−09	−24	−43	−30	36	−16	−02		03	41	−03	51
Neuroticism	−66	78	40	−49	10	34	02	−03		−81	31	−14
Leadership	63	−77	14	25	10	−38	01	46	−84		−35	24
Creativity	−44	07	02	38	−17	59	39	−04	33	−35		62
School achievement	−20	−33	19	37	−01	26	37	47	−10	20	63	

Table 4.17: 16PF (Form C) second order factors, derived criteria, NSQ total and IAS total intercorrelations

Females N = 609 (upper triangle) · Male N = 549 (lower triangle)

	Exvia	Anxiety	Cortertia	Independence	Discreetness	Prodigal subjectivity	Intelligence	Super ego strength	Neuroticism	Leadership	Creativity	School achievement	NSQ total	IAS total
Exvia		−20	45	17	−34	35	−06	−08	−42	53	−49	−31	−39	−23
Anxiety	−19		−10	−15	21	19	07	−12	85	−72	07	−28	46	73
Cortertia	16	−07		21	−10	28	−14	−03	−35	47	−17	−20	−31	−05
Independence	43	−25	23		−40	35	−03	−48	−16	−11	58	18	−31	08
Discreetness	−39	26	−30	−29		10	02	24	23	−07	−21	−02	30	12
Prodigal subjectivity	−21	06	−10	15	−04		11	−17	22	−04	23	−17	−04	09
Intelligence	09	01	09	−04	04	11		03	00	07	31	39	02	09
Super ego strength	−19	−05	−27	−38	16	−25	00		−08	46	−22	53	28	−27
Neuroticism	−54	80	−32	−42	33	32	00	03		−80	29	−17	51	62
Leadership	59	−69	18	21	−23	−45	06	37	−82		−37	23	−35	−63
Creativity	−38	00	09	43	−11	64	39	−08	24	−28		43	09	21
School achievement	−35	−28	−14	17	−01	24	45	46	−11	16	54		07	−22
NSQ Total	−51	42	−35	−31	32	37	10	21	60	−50	30	20		36
IAS Total	−19	76	−03	−11	29	15	04	−20	61	−63	09	−23	36	

Table 4.18: 16PF (Form D) second order factors, derived criteria, NSQ total and IAS total intercorrelations

Females N = 609

Male N = 549

	Exvia	Anxiety	Cortertia	Independence	Discreetness	Prodigal subjectivity	Intelligence	Super ego strength	Neuroticism	Leadership	Creativity	School achievement	NSQ total	IAS total
Exvia		-22	47	12	-32	25	-03	-01	-48	60	-50	-26	-36	-21
Anxiety	-26		-17	-26	30	11	-01	-03	79	-71	-09	-29	47	71
Cortertia	16	-15		23	-10	10	-09	-07	-47	50	-22	-26	-34	-06
Independence	35	-39	30		-32	18	03	-48	-21	-08	60	26	-34	04
Discreetness	-23	21	-18	-22		14	02	07	33	-19	-15	-12	21	15
Prodigal subjectivity	-23	-04	-26	08	-12		-05	06	26	00	27	08	08	01
Intelligence	-04	00	05	-02	03	03		-06	-08	10	23	30	-03	-04
Super ego strength	-21	-02	-37	-43	09	-05	06		06	00	-14	45	36	-16
Neuroticism	-60	77	-46	-43	22	33	-04	12		-78	28	-03	55	55
Leadership	59	-71	18	17	-13	-36	13	36	-80		-33	14	-36	-59
Creativity	-43	-12	-07	44	-17	62	30	02	27	-23		55	07	07
School achievement	-29	-33	-20	24	-13	40	43	46	-03	18	64		19	-20
NSQ Total	-52	44	-42	-45	14	34	05	41	64	-43	22	25		36
IAS Total	-20	77	-14	-20	17	05	-03	-11	63	-62	-01	-23	36	

multiple correlations for both sexes for Exvia and Anxiety with the Leadership derived criterion are of the order of 0.8 which, as we have noted earlier, is as high if not higher than the alternate form reliabilities of the variables in question. This suggests that 'Leaders' in Cattell's terms are simply stable extraverts. It may be that good leaders are indeed low on anxiety and high on extraversion (the latter is open to more argument than the former) but this must be open to empirical validation. Whatever the case, knowing the relationship between the first two Cattell second orders and this particular derived criterion will save the user considerable computational effort.

The Neuroticism derived criterion shows very high positive relationship with Anxiety and negative correlation with Exvia; findings which suggest that neurotics in Cattell's terms, are anxious introverts. 'Neurotics' then, demonstrate the very opposite personality characteristics of 'Leaders' which is reflected in the negative correlations of approximately 0.80 between these two dimensions. The two remaining derived criteria of Creativity and School Achievement are less closely related to Exvia and Anxiety and there is some positive relationship between them.

Chapter 5

Comparability of the Eysenck and Cattell Scales

To the assiduous reader of the psychological journals, the controversy which has from time to time variously raged and simmered between the schools of Eysenck and Cattell, and most especially between their eponymous leaders, will be only too familiar. Whilst both are essentially trait psychologists and look to factor analysis as an important technique in the development of their theoretical models, Cattell and Eysenck differ as to the number and type of factors which they consider to be most efficiently descriptive of human personality. In this chapter, after a brief introduction to the debate, we shall consider what light our results can throw on this question.

Cattell's taxonomy of personality traits has a long and complex history. Beginning with studies of ratings ('L' data), that is to say the assignment of scores on traits by a small group of individuals to larger groups of subjects, Cattell proceeded by a combination of cluster and factor analyses to the identification of 12 primary dimensions of personality. Subsequent investigations using the questionnaire technique added a number of further factors to this list, and whilst it has been suggested that as many as 20 or more primary factors ('source traits') may be identifiable, the 16 factors with which the user of the 16PF is familiar were chosen as the most important dimensions for the construction of the questionnaire. The original studies using the rating technique are described in Cattell (1946); for a very full discussion of the development of Cattell's factor system and theory of personality, Cattell (1957) should be consulted. The most up to date exposition of his views is to be found in Cattell (1973).

Whereas Cattell is an Englishman who has made his home in America, Eysenck is of German origin, but has espoused the methods characteristic of British empiricism. Both men studied natural science as undergraduates; both acknowledge their indebtedness to Spearman, whose work laid the foundations for modern factor analytic methods. Whilst Cattell has studied physiological measures and other objective ('T') techniques parallel with his work on questionnaires and ratings, and claims considerable success in cross-matching from one medium to the other, Eysenck's approach is cast more in the classical experimental mould. His identification of two orthogonal (i.e. uncorrelated) dimensions, extraversion–introversion and neuroticism–stability (with possibly a third dimension of psychoticism) is linked with experimental studies in the laboratory as well as with the use of factor analytic methods.

The great divide between Eysenck and Cattell is on the question of the amount of credence to be given to Cattell's first order factors. In Cattell's view, Eysenck has extracted too few factors and thereby lost useful information; in Eysenck's view Cattell has extracted too many factors, which have proved to be neither replicable nor invariant across the sexes. The latest shots in this campaign are to be found in Eysenck (1972) and Cattell (1972): Eysenck and Eysenck (1969) present a number of studies concerning the factor structure of both the EPI and the 16PF.

Our own study involved the administration of the Eysenck Personality Inventory (Form A) along with Forms C and D of the 16PF and the IPAT Anxiety Scale and Neuroticism Scale Questionnaire to half the students in the sample. Our intention was to examine the relationship between the two sets of scales: other researchers have found close correspondence between Eysenck's Extraversion (E) factor and Cattell's second order Exvia, and between Cattell's second order Anxiety and Eysenck's Neuroticism, (N): we fully expect to replicate this result. However, as this study involved administration of the complete questionnaires rather than a sample of marker items from each, as has been the case in previous work, and furthermore also yields estimates of the reliability of the scales, we are in a position to discover whether in fact Cattell's first order factors carry more information than Eysenck's two factors. Thus the handicaps under which Eysenck (1972) laboured and which gave scope for Cattell's (1972) rebuttal are avoided.

Correlations between the 16PF and the EPI

The correlations between Eysenck's factors and Cattell's first order factors are given in Table 5.1 and those between Eysenck's factors and Cattell's second order factors, derived criteria scales and the IAS and NSQ totals are given in Table 5.2.

Table 5.1: Correlation of 16PF first order factors with the Eysenck Extraversion and Neuroticism Scales

		A	B	C	E	F	G	H	I	L	M	N	O	Q1	Q2	Q3	Q4
FEMALES N=609																	
Form C	E	37	−05	15	32	59	−27	58	07	11	−01	−21	−22	10	−33	−18	09
	N	−16	11	−58	04	−21	−05	−32	04	21	11	16	58	09	12	−32	57
Form D	E	38	−05	12	28	53	−26	46	−08	11	−10	−10	−13	26	−21	−23	−02
	N	−05	−04	−59	−01	−16	03	−32	−02	21	07	15	61	03	10	−31	53
C + D	E	43	−06	16	36	66	−31	57	−01	14	−07	−21	−21	22	−32	−25	04
	N	−12	05	−68	02	−21	−01	−35	01	27	11	20	69	07	13	−37	65
MALES N=549																	
Form C	E	36	−13	16	40	58	−27	58	−10	12	−09	−31	−17	10	−38	−14	03
	N	−11	04	−57	−01	−06	−01	−31	05	21	05	29	68	05	11	35	64
Form D	E	36	−11	10	35	57	−29	44	−18	06	−10	−07	−15	30	−27	−26	−04
	N	−01	−03	−62	00	−09	07	−30	01	21	−02	13	64	−07	02	−25	62
C + D	E	41	−15	15	44	68	−32	57	−16	11	−12	−27	−18	24	−40	−24	00
	N	−07	01	−68	−01	−29	03	−34	04	26	02	29	74	−01	−08	−35	72
TOTAL N = 1158																	
Form C	E	36	−09	16	36	59	−27	58	−02	12	−05	−26	−19	10	−35	−16	05
	N	−13	08	−57	02	−14	−01	−31	11	20	10	23	65	07	10	−34	62
Form D	E	37	−08	11	31	54	−27	45	−13	09	−10	−09	−14	28	−24	−24	−03
	N	−01	−03	−60	−03	−15	06	−31	05	19	05	13	64	−04	06	−27	59
C + D	E	42	−11	15	39	66	−31	57	−08	12	−09	−24	−19	23	−36	−24	02
	N	−08	03	−67	−03	−17	02	−35	09	24	09	24	73	02	10	−36	70

Table 5.2: Correlation of the 16PF second order factors and derived criteria with the Eysenck Extraversion and Neuroticism Scales

		Exvia	Anxiety	Corter-tia	Indepen-dence	Discreet-ness	Prodigal subjec-tivity	Intell-igence	Super-ego	Neurot-icism	Leader-ship	Creat-ivity	School achieve-ment
FEMALES N = 609													
Form C	E	68	−14	38	25	−28	31	−05	−35	−28	26	−25	−38
	N	−24	74	−13	03	10	05	13	−15	64	−61	20	−13
Form D	E	62	−13	35	25	−21	15	−04	−35	−33	25	−25	−37
	N	−20	71	−14	−04	12	−01	−04	−08	57	−57	02	−15
C + D	E	70	−13	41	28	−31	28	−05	−40	−35	28	−30	−44
	N	−22	77	−12	00	16	06	05	−13	66	−64	12	−18
MALES N = 549													
Form C	E	73	−10	16	32	−35	−14	−13	−30	−35	32	−30	−39
	N	−21	77	−09	−21	27	10	06	−09	63	−60	04	−21
Form D	E	68	−11	14	29	−12	−18	−11	−36	−38	26	−33	−37
	N	−19	75	−14	−25	13	00	−01	00	58	−54	−05	−17
C + D	E	77	−10	21	34	−33	−17	−16	−39	−42	31	−38	−44
	N	−21	80	−13	−25	27	06	02	−05	64	−62	−01	−26
TOTAL N = 1158													
Form C	E	70	−12	26	28	−32	11	−09	−33	−31	29	−27	−38
	N	−22	76	−16	−08	20	01	10	−10	64	−59	13	−17
Form D	E	64	−12	23	26	−16	00	−07	−36	−35	25	−29	−37
	N	−19	69	−19	−11	12	−06	−03	−03	56	−53	00	−15
C + D	E	73	−12	29	31	−31	07	−11	−40	−38	30	−34	−44
	N	−21	77	−18	−10	19	01	03	−09	64	−62	08	−21

It is immediately apparent from Table 5.2 that these correlations lend strong support to the suggestion that the 16PF Exvia and Anxiety are the counterparts of the EPI Extraversion and Neuroticism factors, arrived at by different means. The correlation between Cattell's versions of these dimensions is in fact slightly stronger than that between Eysenck's versions (round about −.2 as opposed to −.08); that is to say, they fit slightly less well Eysenck's model of ideally orthogonal factors, but the difference is not so large as to cast doubt on the identification. The correlations between Exvia and Extraversion and between Anxiety and Neuroticism are all of the order of .7 to .8, in other words, of the same magnitude as the alternate form reliabilities of Cattell's first two second order factors and those reported by Eysenck and Eysenck (1964) for the EPI. This suggests that Exvia is the direct equivalent of Extraversion and Anxiety of Neuroticism. That is to say, there is a fundamental agreement between the two sets of scales that there exist two broad influences in personality.

The correlations between the EPI and the IAS and NSQ are given in Table 5.3. It is clear that Eysenck's Neuroticism is highly related to the IAS total score. In view of the high correlation between the IAS and the 16PF second order Anxiety noted in Chapter 4 and a similarly strong relationship between Anxiety and Eysenck's N mentioned above, this is perhaps only to be expected. Cattell's Neuroticism Scale Questionnaire on the other hand is significantly correlated with both the EPI *E* and *N* Factors. This seems to indicate that those scoring highly on Cattell's Neuroticism would fall into the unstable introvert quadrant of Eysenck's typology.

Table 5.3: Correlations between the EPI and the IAS and NSQ

EPI	Females		Males		Total	
	IAS	*NSQ*	*IAS*	*NSQ*	*IAS*	*NSQ*
E	−06	−51	−05	−52	−05	−48
N	75	42	75	44	78	46

Table 5.4: Percentages of reliable variance in 16PF first order factors not accounted for by Eysenck's E and N

	A	B	C	E	F	G	H	I	L	M	N	O	Q1	Q2	Q3	Q4
Females																
Form C	62	90	11	66	−12	79	18	98	74	95	44	03	94	65	57	17
Form D	64	97	09	75	12	82	42	98	74	94	75	00	77	85	51	32
Form C+D	63	98	10	70	01	80	31	1.00	72	96	62	03	87	76	54	21
Males																
Form C	64	93	23	57	03	81	12	97	74	95	−64	00	95	34	61	03
Form D	68	94	12	67	06	78	43	91	80	95	80	12	68	68	58	11
Form C+D	68	94	17	61	03	81	29	95	77	95	20	06	86	51	59	07
Males and females																
Form C	65	93	18	62	−04	81	15	97	75	95	−02	01	95	56	55	05
Form D	66	96	12	72	11	81	42	95	80	95	79	06	73	79	57	16
Form C+D	69	96	16	68	05	81	29	97	79	96	45	04	87	68	57	09

Table 5.5: Percentages of reliable variance in 16PF second order factors not accounted for by Eysenck's E and N

	Exvia	Anxiety	Corter-tia	Indepen-dence	Discreet-ness	Prodigal subject-ivity	Intell-igence	Super-ego strength	Neurot-icism	Leader-ship	Creat-tivity	School achieve-ment
Females												
Form C	−06	05	92	69	−46	93	91	78	10	22	77	38
Form D	08	09	91	70	77	91	94	72	17	39	19	48
Form C+D	01	09	89	71	21	94	92	72	15	31	72	40
Males												
Form C	09	10	59	85	45	62	88	66	10	27	76	38
Form D	26	17	65	86	64	92	98	71	28	36	84	89
Form C+D	19	15	65	93	55	78	98	67	16	31	81	41
Males and Females												
Form C	04	03	80	81	04	96	91	73	10	27	82	40
Form D	21	20	81	83	73	99	97	71	22	42	78	45
Form C+D	12	13	80	91	47	99	96	69	18	32	77	42

Table 5.6: Unique reliable variance in 16PF first order factors expressed as a percentage of total scale variance

	A	B	C	E	F	G	H	I	L	M	N	O	Q1	Q2	Q3	Q4
Females																
Form C	17	03	03	11	−02	19	08	16	06	10	01	01	15	13	10	04
Form D	18	03	02	13	02	20	18	16	06	10	02	00	12	16	10	08
Form C+D	18	03	02	12	00	19	13	16	06	10	01	01	14	15	10	05
Males																
Form C	19	10	07	14	01	22	04	23	09	07	−01	00	14	03	11	01
Form D	20	10	03	16	01	21	15	22	10	07	01	04	10	06	11	03
Form C+D	20	10	05	15	01	22	10	23	09	07	00	02	12	05	11	02
Males and Females																
Form C	18	06	05	13	−01	21	06	24	07	09	00	00	14	08	10	01
Form D	19	06	03	15	02	21	16	24	07	09	02	02	11	11	10	04
Form C+D	19	06	04	14	01	21	11	24	07	09	01	01	13	10	10	02

Table 5.7: Unique reliable variance in 16PF second order factors and derived criteria expressed as a percentage of total scale variance

	Exvia	Anxiety	Cortertia	Independence	Discreetness	Prodigal subjectivity	Intelligence	Superego strength	Neuroticism	Leadership	Creativity	School achievement
Females												
Form C	05	06	15	29	02	08	03	24	04	14	21	05
Form D	13	10	16	29	03	11	04	26	11	18	23	05
Form C+D	10	09	16	31	02	10	04	24	07	10	22	05
Males												
Form C	−03	03	26	23	−01	23	08	29	05	11	21	07
Form D	04	05	26	24	02	23	08	27	08	19	05	09
Form C+D	00	05	25	24	01	24	08	27	07	15	19	08
Males and Females												
Form C	02	02	25	27	00	19	06	26	04	13	22	06
Form D	11	11	25	28	02	02	06	26	10	20	21	07
Form C+D	06	07	25	31	02	20	06	25	08	16	21	07

To make the relationship between Eysenck's and Cattell's scales clearer, Tables 5.4 and 5.5 have been prepared from Tables 5.1 and 5.2 as follows: first the correlations in Tables 5.1 and 5.2 were corrected for attenuation, by dividing each correlation by the geometric mean of the reliabilities of the scales involved. This provides an estimate of the underlying correlations between two variables given totally reliable scales. The multiple correlation of the Eysenck factors with each of the Cattell scales was then calculated, the result squared and subtracted from 1. The resulting figures, as entered in Tables 5.4 and 5.5 represent the percentage of systematic (reliable) variance on each 16PF scale not accounted for by Eysenck's factors. Occasionally negative values appear in the tables: these indicate that a better estimate of scores on this 16PF scale in this form is obtainable from some combination of EPI factors than from that scale's own alternate form.

These tables are most illuminating: essentially, given the congruence of *E* and *N* with Exvia and Anxiety, we have two reference coordinates on the approximate nature and relationship of which Cattell and Eysenck are in fundamental agreement. As they are based on independent data, however, we may adopt Eysenck's factors as apt reference points and make inferences concerning Cattell's factors which would not be possible otherwise.

Firstly, let us examine the claim that Cattell's first order factors reveal detail which is obscured by Eysenck's two-factor system. As regards factors C,O and Q4, which are the major factors combining to define the second order Anxiety factor, there seem to be no grounds at all to suggest that they have a clear and separate identity as represented in these scales. Of the three, only Factor C shows signs of unique variance across the sexes, and even then the percentage involved is small indeed.

On the other hand, the primary source traits contributing to the second order Exvia factor show a degree of robust uniqueness. Whilst Factor F and possibly Factor H seem to be more or less accounted for by Extraversion, Factors A, E, G and Q2 show a good proportion of systematic variance which is independent of *E* and *N*. The factors which seem to be totally independent of Eysenck's *E* and *N* are Factor I and Factor Q1, with Factor Q3 showing moderate independence.

The case of Factors I and Q1 are of particular interest, since these are characterized by Cattell as concerning a tough-minded/tender-minded distinction in the first case and conservatism/radicalism in the second. Essentially similar descriptions of social attitudes bearing similar names and labelled T and R respectively are to be found in Eysenck (1960). The difference between the two schools may on this point be merely a matter of semantics.

The other factors which from Table 5.3 may look particularly robust are B, L, M and N, but this robustness is somewhat illusory. Remembering that the values given are the percentages of *systematic* variance not accounted for by Eysenck's factors, a glance at Table 4.1 which gives their reliabilities should dispel the illusion. There is in fact so little systematic variance at all associated with these scales (less than 10 per cent of scale variance is reliable) that the independence of what there is from E and N is hardly very significant. Misinterpretation can be avoided by consulting Tables 5.6 and 5.7 which give the percentage for each 16PF scale of variance which is both reliable and unique (i.e. not predictable from the EPI). Notice particularly the odd behaviour of Factor N in Table 5.4; Eysenck's E and N together account for more of 16PF Factor N form C for males than does Factor N 16PF Form D, which itself is subsequentially independent of E and N. Things are a little more stable with Factor N in females, but combining the sexes gives the very odd result that Factor N Form C is totally accounted for by Eysenck's factors whereas Factor N Form D is largely independent of them. The circumstantial evidence of the relatively stable relationship between alternate forms of the same factor across sexes with E and N for most of the other factors in the 16PF should suffice to make the point that Cattell's scales, rather than Eysenck's, are behaving oddly here.

We leave it to the reader to inspect the pattern of results for the other first order factors in Table 5.3, and to notice how certain factors on each form relate differentially to Eysenck's scales.

As regards the second order factors and derived criteria, we have already commented on the correspondence between Exvia and Anxiety and E and N. We take no side in the dispute as to whether the factor which Cattell calls Anxiety and Eysenck calls Neuroticism is properly called by one name or the other. Readers interested in this particular controversy are referred to Cattell and Scheier (1961). Discreetness (QV) behaves in the same odd way as Factor N, which is not altogether surprising as Factor N is by far the largest contributor to this second order factor.

With the second order factors, as with the primary source traits, it should be borne in mind that much of the variance in each scale is not reliable, true variance: the data in Tables 5.3 and 5.4 may give the misleading impression that a strong reliable factor independent of the Eysenck factors is represented by the scales concerned. To get the proportion of total scale variance which is reliable and unique it is necessary to consult Tables 5.6 and 5.7, where the figure in Tables 5.3 or 5.4 has been multiplied by the square of the alternate form reliability coefficient.

These results have a bearing on the re-current argument between Eysenck and Cattell as to the possibility of reliable measurement of first order factors. On the one hand, Cattell does not appear to have succeeded in breaking down the second order Anxiety factor into separable first order factors. However intuitively appealing it may be to discuss different forms and components of anxiety, and however successful experimental studies of one kind or another may be, given that anxiety is operationally defined as that which is measured by the questionnaire scale, it is clear that C, O and Q4 are not clearly distinct from one another and from the second order scale to which they contribute. For the interpreter of questionnaire scores to place differential significance on scores on these scales must for the moment be regarded as tendentious.

With regard to Exvia, however, the situation is somewhat different. For example, Cattell's Factor A, an important contributor to Exvia, is, as may be seen from Table 5.4, substantially independent of Extraversion: Factors F and H are very much less so. In this case at least, Cattell's claim that there is information to be found in first order factors which will be obscured if only second orders are used seems justified.

Finally, it is undoubtedly the case that the scales of the 16PF cover ground which is ignored by the EPI, notably the tender-minded / tough-minded and the conservative / radical dimensions, along with intelligence.

Arbitrary factoring

In our discussion of the relationship between Eysenck's and Cattell's factors so far, we have taken what is essentially a bivariate approach; given that the EPI factors are to all intents and purposes orthogonal, we can convert correlations between EPI scales and 16PF scales into proportions of variance and see to what extent the EPI factors account for 16PF factors.

As always when using bivariate techniques with multivariate data, this approach leaves important questions unanswered. In particular in this instance there is the matter of the extent to which Eysenck's factors account for the covariances between Cattell's scales.

Among the most important criteria for accepting the outcome of a factor analysis, is the requirement that the original correlation matrix should as nearly as possible be reproducible from the obtained solution. Put another way, this means that the residual matrix remaining after the extraction of an appropriate number of factors should be a close approximation to a diagonal matrix. The diagonal elements will in general be non-zero since the unreliability of the variables entered will lead to unique ('error') variance remaining after the extraction of all common variance. Thus an appropriate test of the respective claims of Eysenck and Cattell is to extract from an intercorrelation matrix of EPI and 16PF scales two factors targeted so as to exhaust the columns and rows associated with EPI factors. Inspection of the effect of this procedure on the remainder of the matrix will then yield an impression of the extent to which Eysenck's factors span the same space as Cattell's.

Fortunately the orthogonality of Eysenck's scales make this task relatively straightforward. A method is available (Cooley and Lohnes, 1972) for the extraction of arbitrary orthogonal factors targeted on particular variables. The method is essentially sequential: the first targeted factor exhausts the row and column associated with the variable on which it is targeted; the second is placed orthogonal to the first, and likewise exhausts the relevant row and column, and so on. Note that due to the orthogonality of successive factors, where non-zero correlations exist between variables on which factors are to be targeted the resultant factors will not, with the exception of the first, be strictly co-linear with the variables on which they are targeted. This becomes increasingly important as more factors are extracted.

The extraction of Eysenck's E and N from a matrix of inter-correlations between EPI and 16PF scales fits this model very neatly. The correlation between E and N is so slight as to make only one *caveat* necessary in the interpretation of the results: the EPI scales will seem to account for very slightly more of the matrix than in fact they do.

Arbitrary factoring has been employed here because it is a far better device for hypothesis testing than conventional methods of factor analysis. Rather than derive new factor solutions and become heavily involved in argument over the precise techniques used in such an analysis, with arbitrary factoring we can more directly test the hypothesis, for example, that the EPI can account for all the reliable variance in the 16PF. If this hypothesis is rejected it is possible to continue to extract the variance associated with other scales until all reliable variance has been exhausted. That is, we can test how well various theoretical models as represented by these personality scales fit the data.

The computer program provided by Cooley and Lohnes (*op. cit.*) was modified somewhat so as to yield proportions only of 16PF variance extracted by EPI targeted factors and several analyses performed. Analyses were performed variously by sex, entering 16PF Form C and D factors separately (32 variables) or added together (16 variables) and so forth. The results of all these analyses are in close agreement: taken together, EPI Form A Extraversion and Neuroticism scales account for 20 to 23 per cent of the variance of the 16PF factors, the higher figures being associated with males, the lower with females, when Forms C + D scales are used, and around 16 per cent when Forms C and Form D scales are entered separately. Replacing the unities in the diagonal of the correlation matrix with alternate form reliabilities does not increase these proportions beyond the second decimal place. These proportions are considerably smaller than we had anticipated: There is clearly a good deal of reliable variance in the 16PF which is unaccounted for. Table 5.8 gives the total sexes alternate form reliability of the C and D scales reduced by the extraction of EPI, E and N.

The next step, clearly, was to continue the process of extracting arbitrary factors, picking at each stage the 16PF scale which had the lowest communality with the factors so far extracted until the orthogonality restriction made further factors uninterpretable.

The results of this procedure fit pre-existing theory almost too neatly: Factor B, as one would expect, was the first factor to be extracted, followed by Factor I and Factor Q1, that is to say Intelligence, Tough/Tender-mindedness, Conservatism/Radicalism. The five factors thus extracted account for a total of 42 to 45 per cent of the variance of the 16 C + D factors, or 35 to 37 per cent of the variance of the 32 C & D factors entered separately.

At this stage the matrix is still far from diagonal — that is to say there is still scope for further analysis. In particular, Factor A remains strong, having a reduced alternate form reliability in excess of .35 at this stage; factors G and Q3 remain substantial (their reduced intercorrelation is still as high as .4) and even factors C, O and Q4, which might have been expected to be annihilated by the extraction of Neuroticism, retain a crop of residual correlations over .1. A typical table of alternate form reliabilities after the extraction of 5 factors (EPI E & N, 16PF Factors B, I, Q1) is presented in Table 5.9.

The conclusion is inescapable, therefore; even with the shorter less reliable forms of the 16PF, many more than two factors are to be found. Extraversion and Neuroticism, whilst clearly important, are not even exhaustive when referred to the reliable variance of the 16PF scales to which they are analogous. In particular, Cattell's Factor A is not as closely identifiable with Extraversion as might be supposed. Nor is an 'Eysenckian' five-factor model exhaustive: However unreliable the scales, it seems clear that there is reliable variance associated with 16PF factors beyond that accounted for by Extraversion, Neuroticism, Intelligence, Tender-mindedness and Conservatism.

At this point the obvious factor to extract would be G (Super-ego Strength). Unfortunately, by this stage the communality of Factor G with the five-factor model was such that a factor targeted

Table 5.8: Alternate form reliabilities of the 16PF after extraction of EPI Extraversion and Neuroticism

A	B	C	E	F	G	H	I	L	M	N	O	Q1	Q2	Q3	Q4
.409	.252	.164	.367	.124	.434	.290	.494	.253	.293	.096	.127	.363	.290	.293	.148

Table 5.9: Alternate form reliabilities of the 16PF after extraction of the five factor model

A	B	C	E	F	G	H	I	L	M	N	O	Q1	Q2	Q3	Q4
.366	00	.161	.321	.120	.421	.273	00	.251	.103	.090	.126	00	.264	.288	.139

on it would necessarily be inaccurate, due to the orthogonality restriction of the program. Other methods are being adopted to pursue this point and it is hoped to report on these analyses elsewhere at a later date.

The Motivational Distortion and Lie Scales

As we have seen with regard to the factor scales of the EPI and 16PF, part of the difficulty in making reasonable comparisons is terminological rather than substantive. Authors attach different meanings to words: we may find what is for all practical purposes the same concept differently expressed, or different concepts represented by the same words. Thus, for example, the lack of agreement between Eysenck and Cattell as to the nature of neuroticism has made our discussion the more difficult, in that we have had to distinguish Neuroticism in Eysenck's sense, which aligns most closely with Anxiety in Cattell's system, from Neuroticism as a derived criterion having no close single analogy in the terminology of Eysenck.

Similar difficulties arise with regard to the subsidiary scales devised by the two authors to detect untoward response sets in testees. The implications of the 16PF Motivational Distortion and the EPI Lie Scales are much the same when it comes to interpreting results: a high score suggests that scores on the other scales should not be taken at face value. The methods suggested for the practical application of the results obtained on these scales differs: Eysenck's suggestion is that when the lie score exceeds four or five, the *E* and *N* scores should be regarded with considerable scepticism. Cattell on the other hand suggests a series of approximate corrections to apply to the 16PF traits when the MD sten is seven or more.

Table 5.10: Correlation matrices of the 16PF Motivational Distortion scales (MD) and the EPI Lie Scale

		MD Scale 16PF Form C	MD Scale 16PF Form D	MD Scale 16PF Form C + D	Lie Scale EPI
			FEMALES n = 609		
	MD Scale 16PF Form C		89	97	38
MALES N = 549	MD Scale 16PF Form D	89		97	38
	MD Scale 16PF Form C + D	97	97		39
	Lie Scale EPI	36	39	39	

The correlation matrix of the 16PF Motivational Distortion scales (which are only to be found in Forms C and D of the questionnaire) and the EPI Lie Scale is given in Table 5.10. Male undergraduates are represented above and female undergraduates below the main diagonal. As is to be expected with scales of similar item content, there is a high correlation (.89) for both sexes between MD Form C and MD Form D of the 16PF. The statistical relationship between MD and Eysenck's Lie Scale, however, appears less strong than we might first have expected on purely semantic grounds.

Tables 5.11 and 5.12 show the correlations of the Motivational Distortion and Lie Scales with the various personality scale scores. The strongest relationships with the MD scale involve factors C, O, Q3, and Q4; much as one might expect given Cattell's suggestions for correcting obtained scores for motivational distortion (Cattell, 1972). These, it will be noticed, are the main contributors to the second order Anxiety factors which accounts for the correlation of −.39 between MD and Anxiety scores. The correlations between the EPI Lie Scale and the various personality traits show a remarkably similar pattern.

Splitting the sample into four groups by sex and discipline yields the results presented in Table 5.13. The differences between the mean scores of the four groups are not all statistically significant: nonetheless these results are characterized by the same rank-ordering of groups as was found for scores on the personality factors. Notably, the effect of discipline appears to be greater than that of sex.

In the case of the MD scale, the sex difference is significant at the five per cent level, whereas the Lie Scale does not show a significant difference. For both scales the discipline difference is significant at the one per cent level.

The mean Lie Scale scores we obtained are close to those reported by Eysenck in the EPI manual, whereas our sample scored on average over half a standard deviation lower on the MD scale than Cattell's standardization sample. This finding supports our view that the conditions of administration adopted for the fieldwork of this survey were such as to subject our sample to relatively few constraints which might lead to the appearance of untoward motivational states and which might prejudice the value of our findings for normative purposes. An additional point is the finding by Michaelis and Eysenck (1971) that dissimulating motivating conditions can be distinguished from non-motivating conditions by looking at the correlation between the EPI Neuroticism and Lie Scales. Where testing has taken place under conditions favourable to faking, the correlation is typically around −.5, whereas the correlation is lower in conditions of little dissimulation. The correlation between the Lie Scale and Neuroticism of .23 (Table 5.13) is further evidence therefore that response distortion was not high

Table 5.11: Correlations of the Motivational Distortion and Lie Scales with the 16PF first order factors (Forms C + D) total sexes (N = 1158)

	A	B	C	E	F	G	H	I	L	M	N	O	Q1	Q2	Q3	Q4
MD Scale (C + D)	07	−08	39	−11	07	18	15	−05	−26	−09	−20	−28	−06	−15	37	−37
Lie Scale	−03	−04	25	−24	−10	34	00	−02	−24	−03	−08	−16	−12	−06	40	−28

Table 5.12: Correlations of the Motivational Distortion and Lie Scales with the 16PF (FORMS C + D) second orders, derived criteria, EPI, NSQ and IAS total sexes (N = 1158)

	Ex-via	Anx-iety	Cor-teria	Inde-pen-dence	Dis-creet-ness	Pro-digal Sub-jecti-vity	Intel-lig-ence	Super-ego Stren-gth	Neu-roti-cism	Lea-der-ship	Crea-tivi-ty	School Achieve-ment	EPI E	N	IAS	NSQ
MD Scale (C + D)	10	−39	00	−11	−16	−06	−08	25	−30	37	−12	15	−02	−36	−44	−14
Lie Scale	−08	−27	−09	−21	−01	−07	−04	40	−13	26	−05	26	−20	−23	−33	06

Table 5.13: Means and standard deviations of the MD and Lie Scales by sex and discipline

	N	16PF MD Scale		EPI Lie Scale	
		Mean	*SD*	*Mean*	*SD*
Female Arts	426	6.03	2.10	2.53	1.69
Male Arts	251	6.25	2.22	2.71	1.79
Female Science	238	6.43	2.08	2.90	1.71
Male Science	329	6.80	2.21	2.98	1.79

amongst the students participating in the survey.

Cattell (1972) provides provisional correction procedures by means of which 16PF scores can be corrected for the effects of motivational distortion. These, we must assume for lack of an explicit statement on Cattell's part, are based on correlations between the various personality scales and MD scores. Whatever their origin, however, their use implies that the motivational state of the individual taking the test causes unwanted distortion of scores on the personality scales. That is to say, the resultant profile will be distorted in a specific fashion depending on the test-taking situation.

Since our data are correlational, we are not in a position to infer causal relationships between motivational distortion and personality scale scores. However, given the non-stressful circumstances in which our data were collected, it is notable that the strongest relationships between personality scores and MD scores involve precisely those factors whose correction for motivational distortion is suggested by Cattell, to wit C (Ego Strength), O (Guilt Proneness), Q3 (Self-Concept Control) and Q4 (Ergic Tension).

If we take it that our administration involved only those elements conducive to distortion common to all the situations in which personality tests may be administered and none tending to elicit specific attitudinal states, we must consider whether it is reasonable to employ the correction formulae at all. For it would appear that the relationship between certain personality traits and motivational distortion scores persists outside these situations, e.g. job selection, in which the motivation to distort is generally held most likely to operate.

The possibility exists, therefore, that the tendency to distort is itself a personality trait as well as, or maybe instead of, a situationally bound attitude. If this is the case, then to apply the correction factors will result in less dependable results by the unwarranted introduction of extra error variance into scores.

This question clearly calls for investigation in its own right: our results raise the question of whether and, in what circumstances, the MD scale should properly be considered an attitude scale or a personality scale, but they cannot provide the answer.

In conclusion, it should be mentioned that the very moderate correlation between Eysenck's Lie Scale and Cattell's MD scale may be depressed by the mismatch between the two distribution shapes. The mean MD scores for our groups are at or about the centre of the score range, whilst the Lie Scale distributions are highly positively skewed: hence the correlation coefficient may be depressed by the different scaling properties of the two scales.

Summary

What then can we say in summmary about these findings? First, there are clear areas of overlap between Eysenck and Cattell, more especially between Eysenck's *E* and *N* and Cattell's first two second orders of Exvia and Anxiety. Some 16PF scales such as Factor B (Intelligence) and Q2 (Radicalism) Eysenck does not claim to measure in the EPI, and the 16PF could be said to be more comprehensive in consequence. Eysenck would probably retort of course, that in his view these two factors are not in the same domain as his personality variables and that these 16PF primaries are none too reliably measured in any event. We should also mention that the 16PF contains a Tough versus Tender-mindedness Scale (Factor I), which seems to have a parallel in the new Eysenck Personality Questionnaire (1976).

We found little support for Cattell's breakdown of the 16PF anxiety components into sub-factors of C, (Emotionally-Stable), O (Apprehensive) and Q4 (Tense), although it is not inconceivable that they respond differently to state anxiety, a possibility not investigated in this study.

There was some support on the other hand for Cattell's breakdown of the Exvia second order into relatively reliable sub-factors. Moreover, even after extraction of the 5 factor model of personality (Extraversion, Anxiety, Intelligence, Radicalism and Tough-mindedness), a strong Super-ego Strength factor (Factor G and Q VIII) still remained in the 16PF.

Only a moderate relationship was found between the EPI Lie and Motivational Distortion Scales of the 16PF. This could in part be due to the rather different distribution shapes on the two scales.

Finally, the reader should bear in mind that these comparisons between the Eysenck and Cattell Scales have been carried out using the shorter, less reliable forms of the 16PF. It is at least possible that even more unique variance would remain after the extraction of Eysenck's factors from Forms A and B of the 16PF.

Chapter 6

Factored Scales and Academic Achievement

Studies which have sought to relate personality and ability with measures of academic achievement are by no means new to the literature. Indeed they have been too numerous and often too conflicting in their conclusions for us to review them in any detail here. Nevertheless, without wishing to confuse the issues further, we had intended that this survey would provide useful additional information on the relationships between factored personality scales and academic achievement in the university context.

Two approaches have been adopted here. First, on the assumption that university entrance is to some extent a measure of academic achievement in itself, we shall take undergraduates as a criterion group and compare them in terms of personality with young adults in the general population. Of course, there will be social class, work experience and other differences between the two groups, but nevertheless it is hoped that the comparison will shed further light on the personality characteristics of undergraduates. Second, having followed up the students into their third and final year; we shall use degree class as a measure of academic achievement.

Undergraduates compared with young adults

Early in 1972 a study was carried out to standardize the 16PF on the British adult general population. A sample of over 2,000 adults between the ages of 17 and 69 years completed Forms A and B of the 16PF in controlled conditions in their own homes. A full account of the standardization methodology and the characteristics of the sample has been given by Saville (1972a, 1972b).

As part of this study data were collected for approximately 500 young adults in the general population. These results are summarized in Tables 6.1 and 6.2 along with the relevant data for the student samples.

The British undergraduates are of mean age 20 years with 96 per cent of the group in the age range 17 to 24 years and the British young adults of mean age 20 years with a range of 16 to 24 years. It should also be noted that as a cross section of the general population in this group, some 10 per cent of the young adults were university students. Clearly this overlap will tend to reduce the size of the differences between the two groups. Moreover, all the young adults were sufficiently literate to read the questionnaire booklets for themselves.

We begin the analysis by comparing the mean scores on the 16PF first order factors for the groups, broken down by the sex of the respondents. Most of the differences between the two samples are very much in the direction that we would have anticipated. Female undergraduates are significantly lower on factors A,L,N and Q4 and higher on B,C,I,M,Q1 and Q2. There are non-significant differences on the remaining six factors (E,F,G,H,O and Q3).

Table 6.2 presents the results for male undergraduates and young male adults. Again the undergraduates are higher on B,I,M and Q2 and lower on L and N — trends reflected in the data for both sexes combined (Table 6.3). A summary table of the differences between the British young adults and the undergraduate standardization sample is given in Table 6.4.

It is evident from Table 6.4 that the findings are relatively consistent without any dramatic changes in direction across the two sexes. In terms of the trait names provided by Cattell, British university students are more Intelligent (B+), Emotionally stable (C+), Tender-minded (I+), Imaginative (M+), Experimenting (Q1+), and Self-sufficient (Q2+) and *less* Outgoing (A−), Happy-go-lucky (F−), Venturesome (H−), Suspicious (L−), Astute (N−), and Tense (Q4−) than British young adults of the same age.

It is interesting to note that our conclusions regarding the differences between students and young adults vary to some extent, depending on the sex and the particular academic discipline of the students under study. When we take account of the differences between arts and science undergraduates on the 16PF (Chapter 3), we find, for example, that male arts students are significantly more and male science students significantly less Outgoing (Factor A) than the young adult group. In fact only on Factors B,M and N are the results unequivocal when account is taken of variation as a result of the sex and discipline of the students in the university sample.

The pattern emerging from these results, however, is much as one might expect: undergraduates tend to be more intelligent, imaginative and wrapped-up in more abstract concerns and perhaps rather more emotionally mature and self-sufficient. One might reasonably ask whether these differences are characteristic of people of higher

Table 6.1: 16PF personality differences between British undergraduates and young adults: female: Forms A and B

		A	B	C	E	F	G	H	I	L	M	N	O	Q1	Q2	Q3	Q4
British undergraduates (N = 661)	Mean	20.31	18.60	29.70	21.91	30.13	22.07	22.76	26.80	15.64	27.36	18.75	25.78	19.90	19.83	20.49	28.77
	SD	6.58	2.75	7.11	7.72	8.56	6.51	11.39	5.89	5.30	6.09	4.65	7.94	5.91	6.08	6.58	9.32
Young adults (N = 255)	Mean	21.88	14.68	27.82	20.87	31.07	21.89	23.14	24.14	17.29	21.34	20.69	26.34	18.13	18.97	20.02	30.71
	SD	5.16	3.27	6.65	6.50	8.18	5.47	10.49	4.49	5.11	6.04	4.66	7.09	4.81	5.40	5.67	7.38
Differences in means (positive if undergraduates higher)		−1.57	3.92	1.88	1.04	−.94	.18	−.38	2.66	−1.65	6.02	−1.94	−.56	1.77	.86	.47	−1.94
t value		3.42	18.31	3.65	1.91	1.51	.39	.46	6.51	4.26	13.43	5.65	.98	4.27	1.98	1.00	2.98
Significance of difference p <		.01	.01	.01	NS	NS	NS	NS	.01	.01	.01	.01	NS	.01	.05	NS	.01

Table 6.2: 16PF personality differences between British undergraduates and young adults: male: Forms A and B

		A	B	C	E	F	G	H	I	L	M	N	O	Q1	Q2	Q3	Q4
British undergraduates (N = 595)	Mean	17.96	18.23	31.09	27.20	29.61	21.64	24.40	20.35	17.50	27.50	17.63	21.12	21.52	20.59	22.20	24.30
	SD	6.92	2.94	7.60	7.58	9.39	6.69	11.95	6.87	5.40	6.54	4.52	8.69	5.58	6.22	6.69	9.59
Young adults (N = 234)	Mean	18.04	15.02	30.48	26.77	32.67	21.07	28.56	17.02	18.89	23.32	18.78	20.47	21.57	18.85	21.57	25.54
	SD	5.70	3.02	7.13	7.35	8.43	6.14	10.21	6.11	5.32	5.83	4.63	8.32	5.03	5.84	6.09	9.24
Differences in means (Positive if undergraduates higher)		−.08	3.21	.61	.43	−3.06	.57	−4.16	3.33	−1.39	4.18	−1.15	.65	−.05	1.74	.63	−1.24
t value		.16	14.03	1.06	.74	4.34	1.13	4.69	6.47	3.35	8.53	3.27	.98	.12	3.68	1.25	1.69
Significance of difference p <		NS	.01	NS	NS	.01	NS	.01	.01	.01	.01	.01	NS	NS	.01	NS	NS

Table 6.3: 16PF personality differences between British undergraduates and young adults: female and male: Forms A and B

		A	B	C	E	F	G	H	I	L	M	N	O	Q1	Q2	Q3	Q4
British undergraduates (N = 1256)	*Mean*	19.20	18.42	30.36	24.42	29.89	21.86	23.54	23.74	16.62	27.43	18.22	23.57	20.68	20.19	21.30	26.66
	SD	6.84	2.84	7.37	8.09	8.97	6.60	11.68	7.14	5.45	6.31	4.62	8.62	5.81	6.15	6.68	9.71
Young adults (N = 489)	*Mean*	20.04	14.84	29.09	23.69	31.84	21.50	25.74	20.74	18.05	22.29	19.78	23.53	19.78	18.91	20.76	28.23
	SD	5.74	3.12	7.00	7.51	8.32	5.79	10.68	6.40	5.27	6.02	4.73	8.24	5.20	5.62	5.92	8.70
Differences in means (Positive if undergraduates higher)		−.84	3.58	1.27	.73	−1.95	.36	−2.20	3.00	−1.43	5.14	−1.56	.04	.90	1.28	.54	−1.57
t value		2.40	22.98	3.28	1.73	4.16	1.06	3.62	8.11	4.98	15.48	6.29	.09	2.99	4.00	1.56	3.12
Significance of difference p <		.05	.01	.01	NS	.01	NS	.01	.01	.01	.01	.01	NS	.01	.01	NS	.01

Table 6.4: 16PF personality differences between British undergraduates and young adults: summary table: first order factors Forms A+B

	A	B	C	E	F	G	H	I	L	M	N	O	Q1	Q2	Q3	Q4
Females	Y**	U**	U**	NS	NS	NS	NS	U**	Y**	U**	Y**	NS	U**	U*	NS	Y*
Males	NS	U**	NS	NS	Y**	NS	Y**	U**	Y**	U**	Y**	NS	NS	U**	NS	NS
Males & females	Y*	U**	U**	NS	Y**	NS	Y**	U**	Y**	U**	Y**	NS	U**	U**	NS	Y**

Y: Young Adults significantly higher
U: Undergraduates significantly higher

* p <.05
** p <.01

Figure 6.1: Frequency Polygons of 16PF Factor B Intelligence Scores (Forms A + B)

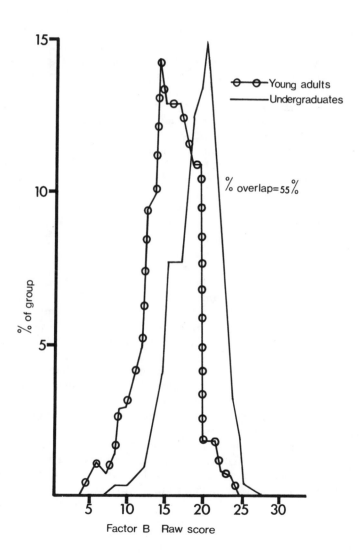

intelligence, or whether the university experience tends to produce a certain precocious maturity. Certainly, if one draws up profiles based on general population adult norms of the mean scores of the two groups, undergraduates and young adults, the undergraduates approximate much more closely to the adult mean than do the non-student young adults.

There is some evidence that a change in scores on personality questionnaires takes place over the first year of an undergraduate course, and it is generally held by university teachers that second-year students are very different as a result of their first year's experience. A longitudinal study on a group of students throughout their university careers might well reveal intriguing shifts.

If for purposes of group description we are to accept the 16PF Forms A and B scores on Factor B as a tolerable measure of intelligence (low reliability may make it unsatisfactory for the assessment of individuals) and if we use the young adults as the base line, it is apparent on a scale of mean 100 and standard deviation 15, that the average undergraduate deviation IQ would be in the region of 120 points. (It should be remembered, however, that the young adults were all capable of reading the questionnaire booklets for themselves so they do not constitute a true cross-section of all young adults in the general population). The overlap between the curves shown in Figure 6.1 is approximately 55 per cent of either curve.

It is interesting that the other major discriminator between the two groups, Factor M, is a non-cognitive scale which Cattell has variously named 'Imagination', 'Inner mental life' and more technically 'Autia'. Accepting the trait labels at face value it would seem that the universities contain a good many impractical students — a point that those outside have not been slow to make in the past! Moreover, as high Factor M has been shown by Suhr (1953) to be related to accident proneness, we may have discovered one reason for the high premiums which car insurance companies typically ask of their student clients!

In addition to the differences in means noted, differences are also evident between undergraduates and the general population young adults with regard to variances, i.e. the overall dispersion of scores on each factor. 'F' ratios have been calculated for each factor: male undergraduates exhibit significantly higher variances on Factors A, F, H, I, M and Q1, female undergraduates on Factors A, E, G, I, O, Q1, Q2, Q3 and Q4. Female undergraduates show significantly less variance than general population young adults on Factor B: for males the difference is in the same direction, but does not reach significance.

Overall, there is a tendency for undergraduates to show more variability on the 16PF than their counterparts in the general population. Sign tests, which give the probability associated with a

Figure 6.2: Frequency Polygon of 16PF Factor M Imagination Scores (Forms A + B)

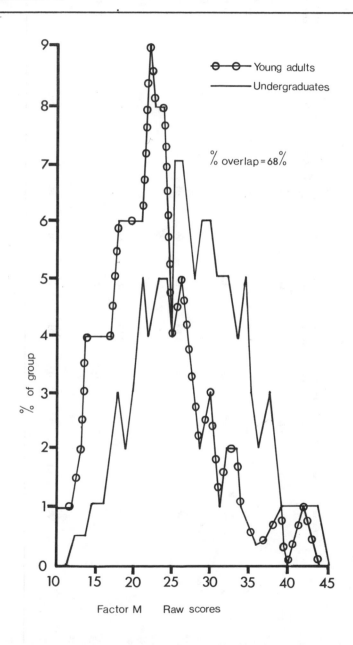

% overlap = 68%

Table 6.5: 16PF personality differences between British undergraduates and young adults: female: Form A second order factors and derived criteria

| | | Second Order Factors | | | | | | | | Derived Criteria | | | |
		Exvia QI	Anxiety QII	Cortertia QIII	Independence QIV	Discreetness QV	Prodigal subjectivity QVI	Intelligence QVII	Superego strength QVIII	Neuroticism	Leadership	Creativity	School achievement
Young adult females (N = 255)	Mean	5.70	6.71	6.02	5.69	6.02	5.97	5.51	4.25	6.03	4.71	5.14	3.76
	SD	1.76	1.63	1.87	1.48	1.94	1.80	1.66	1.86	1.62	1.48	1.52	1.64
Female undergraduates (N = 599)	Mean	5.51	6.17	5.43	6.63	4.97	5.76	7.32	3.85	5.52	4.79	6.50	5.51
	SD	1.95	1.96	2.03	1.76	1.88	2.12	1.66	2.05	2.14	1.92	1.80	1.93
Difference in means (positive if young adults higher)		.19	.54	.59	-.94	1.05	.21	-1.81	.40	.51	-.08	-1.36	-1.75
t value		1.34	3.86	3.97	7.47	7.39	1.38	14.57	2.68	3.41	.59	10.56	12.65
Significance of difference $p <$		NS	.01	.01	.01	.01	NS	.01	.01	.01	NS	.01	.01

Table 6.6: 16PF personality differences between British undergraduates and young adults: female: Form B second order factors and derived criteria

		Second Order Factors									Derived Criteria		
		Exvia	Anxiety	Corter-tia	Indepen-dence	Discreet-ness	Prodigal subject-ivity	Intell-igence	Super-ego strength	Neurot-icism	Leader-ship	Creati-vity	School achieve-ment
		QI	QII	QIII	QIV	QV	QVI	QVII	QVIII				
Young adult females (N = 255)	Mean	5.92	6.14	6.02	5.49	4.66	4.50	6.04	4.62	5.32	5.29	4.95	4.72
	SD	1.76	1.57	1.67	1.78	1.96	1.75	1.75	1.69	1.51	1.57	1.73	1.64
Female undergraduates (N = 599)	Mean	5.51	5.76	4.98	6.38	4.20	4.96	7.88	4.84	5.30	5.28	6.83	6.27
	SD	1.94	1.69	1.98	2.06	1.87	2.06	1.77	1.97	1.71	.1.75	1.95	1.95
Difference in means (positive if young adults higher)		.41	.38	1.04	−.89	.46	−.46	−1.84	−.22	.02	.01	−1.88	−1.55
t value		2.90	3.07	2.56	6.00	3.24	3.12	13.93	1.55	.16	.08	13.31	11.11
Significance of difference p<		.01	.01	.01	.01	.01	.01	.01	NS	NS	NS	.01	.01

Table 6.7: 16PF personality differences between British undergraduates and young adults: male: Form A second order factors and derived criteria

		Second Order Factors									Derived Criteria		
		Exvia QI	Anxiety QII	Corter-tia QII	Indepen-dence QIV	Discreet-ness QV	Prodigal subject-ivity QVI	Intell-igence QVII	Super-ego strength QVIII	Neurot-icism	Leader-ship	Creati-vity	School achieve-ment
Young adult males (N = 234)	Mean	5.65	6.30	5.93	6.26	5.82	5.47	5.65	3.84	5.68	4.78	5.78	4.15
	SD	1.89	1.95	1.86	1.91	1.96	1.85	1.63	1.89	2.10	1.82	1.73	1.98
Male undergraduates (N = 549)	Mean	5.20	6.01	5.82	6.62	5.20	6.51	7.27	3.83	5.68	4.57	6.96	5.99
	SD	2.13	1.98	2.12	1.97	1.98	1.93	1.70	1.95	2.14	1.92	1.80	1.93
Difference in means (positive if young adults higher)		.45	.29	.11	−.36	.62	−1.04	−1.62	.01	–	.21	−1.18	−1.84
t value		2.79	1.88	.69	2.36	4.02	6.98	12.34	.07	–	1.42	8.48	12.10
Significance of difference p<		.01	NS	NS	.01	.01	.01	.01	NS	NS	NS	.01	.01

Table 6.8: 16PF personality differences between British undergraduates and young adults: male: Form B second order factors and derived criteria

| | | Second Order Factors | | | | | | | | Derived Criteria | | | |
		Exvia QI	Anxiety QII	Cortertia QIII	Independence QIV	Discreetness QV	Prodigal subjectivity QVI	Intelligence QVII	Superego strength QVIII	Neuroticism	Leadership	Creativity	School achievement
Young adult males (N = 234)	Mean	5.98	6.18	6.90	6.24	4.51	5.02	6.19	4.24	5.24	5.30	5.59	4.75
	SD	1.72	1.73	2.07	1.76	1.96	2.01	1.75	1.72	1.76	1.81	1.79	1.83
Male undergraduates (N = 549)	Mean	5.31	5.99	6.18	6.65	4.33	6.14	7.61	4.43	5.49	4.95	7.06	6.31
	SD	2.07	1.75	2.18	1.94	2.00	2.19	1.80	1.99	1.85	1.89	1.92	2.01
Difference in means (positive if young adults higher)		.67	.19	.72	−.41	.18	−1.12	−1.42	−.19	−.25	.35	−1.47	−1.56
t value		4.35	1.39	4.29	2.78	1.16	6.70	10.18	1.27	1.75	2.40	9.99	10.19
Significance of difference p <		.001	NS	.01	.01	NS	.01	.01	NS	NS	.01	.01	.01

given set of directions of difference, were performed: for both sexes and for the sexes taken together, undergraduates show significantly higher variability (p <.002).

Differences between the second year undergraduates and young adults on the 16PF second order factors and derived criteria are given in Tables 6.5 to 6.8 and in a summary, Table 6.9, the data having been normed against American N sten norms. The undergraduates can be seen to be significantly lower on Exvia, more Independent and Intelligent and, as we might expect, higher on Cattell's derived criteria of School Achievement and Creativity. They also tend to be higher on Prodigal Subjectivity and Sensitivity and lower on Discreetness. There appear to be few consistent differences on Super-Ego Strength or the derived criteria of Neuroticism and Leadership. (As with other second order data which are based on different weights and norms for the sexes, comparisons should not be made between the results for male and female groups.)

The one factor where a clear sex difference emerges is on Anxiety with no significant differences in males but female undergraduates are of lower measured anxiety than young adult females. This leads us on to the rather conflicting opinions on the role and level of anxiety in the student. Vernon (1964) refers to the 'common finding that college students . . . seem rather more neurotic and introverted than the less educated', whilst Zweig (1964), for example, maintains in *The Student in the Age of Anxiety* that the model student is essentially emotionally stable; the less fortunate student is essentially neurotic whose 'worry is his number one enemy'.

From the data on the main anxiety components of the 16PF (Factors C, O, Q4) and, indeed, the Anxiety second order factor itself, there is certainly no evidence for the undergraduates to be seen as more anxious or unstable in disposition: indeed when sex and academic discipline are taken into consideration the only group which was not significantly lower on the main anxiety factors of the 16PF was male arts students; male and female science and female arts students as groups were all, in fact, lower than young adults of the same sex.

This seems to run counter to much previous research using scales developed by Eysenck (Lynn, 1959; Kelvin *et al.*, 1965; Entwistle, 1972; Child, 1969). Indeed our student mean on the EPI Neuroticism Scale is in fact higher than that reported by Eysenck and Eysenck (1964) for their adult standardization sample. Thus, we are in the rather conflicting position that:

1. When compared with young adults of comparable age, undergraduates are significantly *lower* on Cattell's second order Anxiety scale.

Table 6.9: 16PF personality differences between British undergraduates and young adults: summary table: Forms A / B second order factors and derived criteria

| | Second Order Factors | | | | | | | | Derived Criteria | | | |
	Exvia QI	Anxiety QII	Corter-tia QIII	Indepen-dence QIV	Discreet-ness QV	Prodigal subject-ivity QVI	Intell-igence QVII	Super-ego strength QVIII	Neurot-icism	Leader-ship	Creati-vity	School achieve-ment
Females Form A	NS	Y**	Y**	U**	Y**	NS	U**	Y**	Y**	NS	U**	U**
Females Form B	Y**	Y**	Y**	U**	Y**	Y**	U**	NS	NS	NS	U**	U**
Males Form A	Y**	NS	NS	U**	Y**	U**	U**	NS	NS	NS	U**	U**
Males Form B	Y**	NS	Y**	U**	NS	U**	U**	NS	NS	Y**	U**	U**

Y: Young Adults Significantly higher
U: Undergraduates Significantly higher

* p <.05
** p <.01

2. When compared with general population adults, undergraduates are *higher* on Eysenck's Neuroticism Scale.

A number of explanations for these apparently anomalous results come to mind. There is the possibility that our research procedure attracted a particularly stable group of students. This would go against findings, however, which suggest that it is perhaps the more anxious who volunteer for psychology experiments (Barefoot, 1969). Both the adult and undergraduate groups completed the questionnaire in a research atmosphere, so we do not believe that differences in motivational set are the cause.

The second of the comparisons listed above may be invalidated by the Eysenck general population adult standardization sample which might be described as little more than a rag-bag of various occupational groups. Certainly no clear indication of under what conditions and what circumstances the data were collected is reported. Subjects under employment rather than counselling or research conditions for example will generally project a more favourable impression of themselves by faking towards lower Neuroticism.

Moreover, it is very important to note that EPI *N* scores tend to decrease with age. The higher measured Neuroticism of students then, may merely be the result of the seven year average age difference between undergraduates and Eysenck's adult group. This theory is supported to some extent by the fact that if comparison is made between undergraduates and the total adult sample of mean age 39 years (See Table 3.5.), rather than young adults of mean age 19 years, differences on the main 16PF anxiety components of C, O and Q4 are far less clearcut.

We must not overlook the point of course that the relationship between 16PF second order Anxiety factor and Eysenck's Neuroticism is not perfect. It is feasible that the discrepancy in findings on the anxiety level of students is due to the fact that Cattell's Anxiety is more heavily saturated than Eysenck's Neuroticism with introversion (see Chapter 4) a questionnaire variable on which undergraduates have already been observed to be lower than people in general.

Finally, we would like to suggest that the cause could also lie in the actual time of testing. Whereas many of the studies referred to above were conducted early in the first term of the first year in university, arguably when subjects are in a relatively high state of stress as a result of what is for the majority a radical change in life style, this research was carried out in the second and typically less stressful academic year.

Thus, we are suggesting that results on supposedly trait variables may have been confounded by the situational or 'state' element in anxiety. If this is so it makes it vitally important that the precise conditions, purpose and time of testing are described in any research study.

Whatever the cause, we think that these results militate against any hasty conclusions that undergraduates are more anxious or neurotic than people in general. It is clear that when comparing the personality characteristics of undergraduates with some adult group or other, sex, academic discipline, response style, age and the very nature of the actual scales used, are all important variables to be considered.

Multiple discriminant analyses

The multiple discriminant analysis technique described previously (Chapter 3) in connection with the differences in personality test scores between undergraduates on different courses, was applied to the combined data from this study and the general population sample described by Saville (1972). The undergraduates who had taken Forms A and B of the 16PF were split into four groups by sex and discipline (arts or science). Since approximately ten per cent of the general population sample in this age group were students, it is important to remember that the differences between the groups will be somewhat reduced.

The analysis yielded three significant discriminant functions, of which the first and third, in order of variance accounted for, correspond more or less exactly to the two major discriminant functions found when only undergraduate scores were being analyzed. (See Chapter 3) The First of these is mainly Factor I. The third is more difficult to name, having large contributions from Factors A,E,H and O. The second canonical variate, made up largely of Factor B (Intelligence) and Factor M (Imagination), discriminated more between the general population young adults and the undergraduate sample. On this dimension the undergraduate groups have almost identical mean scores whilst the general population females are furthest removed from them and the general population males lie midway between. On the first and third discriminant functions, the general population groups appear approximately midway between the undergraduate groups of the corresponding sex.

Consequently, it appears that the differences we have noted elsewhere between the disciplines in terms of personality test scores assume an even greater importance. Undergraduate arts student not only appear to be different from their contemporaries in science faculties but the differences are such that, as compared with their counterparts in the general population, the two groups represent in some sense extremes of a continuum. That is to say, that on certain scales, rather than undergraduates as a whole differing from the general population and differing amongst themselves on a somewhat smaller scale, it would seem that with the exception of the Intelligence Factor and Factor M (which is in any case proposed as an 'abstract thinking' factor), science undergraduates are less like arts undergraduates than they are like their fellows in the general population. If this conclusion holds, then the implication for the experimental use of the 16PF is rather surprising: it may matter more with some variables whether student subjects in experiments are arts-based or science-based than whether we choose to use student or general population subjects. This leads us to suspect that just about any study of undergraduates as a whole is likely to run into the same phenomenon. Furthermore, depending on one's views as to how much behavioural variance is predictable from personality tests, we feel that the whole question of choice of specialization is being begged. Perhaps it is assumed too glibly that a student's choice of course is a matter of preference or rational choice between future opportunities rather than a reflection of a more fundamental difference on whose origins we may only, for the moment, speculate.

The relationship between degree class and personality

The next stage of the study involved following up the undergraduates on three year degree courses into their final year and the collection of degree results for the sample. Due to administrative problems, it was not possible to gain the degree results of students from three of the universities which left a group of 1836 individuals. Those students on four-year courses or more, receiving aegrotats, withdrawing from courses or who could not be adequately matched with the main file of data were excluded from the group to leave a final sub-sample of 1395 students.

The sample is made up of final year, full-time degree students on three-year courses. It was decided to include only those students on three-year first degree courses because of the impossibility of measuring degree success at all satisfactorily when results for courses of four years duration or more are included. For example, many five-year courses in medicine have attached to them undivided ordinary degrees which are not directly comparable with the ordinary degrees awarded on most courses of three years' length.

The exact numbers followed up in the Summer of 1974 are given in Table 6.10. The fifth column includes those students who did not receive degree results because of sickness or other reasons. The sixth column refers to unmatched records where record numbers at the time of completing the personality questionnaires did not correspond with those at the time of follow-up or where other data were judged inadequate. Other controls on the quality of the data were carried out such as checking that the degree subject recorded by each student corresponded with the official examination lists.

Table 6.10: Information on the follow-up samples

	Number followed up	Degree results collected	Not on three year degree courses	Withdrawn from course	Degree results unavailable for other reasons	Unmatched records
16PF Forms A+B study	907	705	140	13	13	36
16PF Forms C+D study	929	690	174	13	12	40
Both studies	1836	1395	314	26	25	76

Table 6.11: Degree class distributions for the follow-up samples

		Degree Class				
	Fail	*Pass*	*Third*	*Lower second*	*Upper second*	*First*
16PF A+B Study (N = 705)	1% (7)	7% (46)	9% (60)	42% (295)	35% (250)	6% (44)
16PF C+D Study (N = 690)	1% (7)	7% (51)	7% (52)	43% (299)	33% (230)	7% (51)
Both studies (N = 1395)	1% (14)	7% (97)	8% (112)	43% (594)	34% (480)	7% (95)

A check was made on the representativeness of the follow-up samples (N = 1395) against those not followed-up (N = 1120), by calculating t-tests on the 16PF first order factors for the two groups. It is unnecessary to reproduce the results in full here but in the A/B and C/D studies only one of the differences was significant at the five per cent level and in any case with 32 variables this would have been expected by chance. It seems reasonable to conclude, therefore, that limiting our attention to three-year degree courses seems to have had little appreciable effect on the personality characteristics of the subsample.

The distribution of degree results for the A/B (N = 705) and C/D (N = 690) studies are given in Table 6.11. Of the follow up sample approximately one per cent sat but failed their final examination. This small percentage is identical to that reported by Choppin *et al.* (1973) in their study on some 7000 university undergraduates.

The exact representativeness of the sample in terms of degree class is difficult to establish. We have already noted that students on four-year degree courses have been excluded from our analysis. However, the University Grants Committee (1975) statistics are based on *all* first degrees awarded in any one academic year. In the year 1971/72 (the latest figures available at the time of writing this report) seven per cent of students gained first class degrees, 29 per cent upper second, 37 per cent lower second, 13 per cent other honours and 14 per cent pass or ordinary degrees. This compares reasonably favourably with percentages for the subsample given in Table 6.11, and the lower proportion of pass and ordinary degrees in the sample is very much to be expected.

16PF first order correlations with degree class

Many studies have suggested a linear relationship between certain personality scales and academic performance (Entwistle and Cunningham, 1968; Savage, 1962; Kline, 1966). Accordingly, each of the 16PF first order, second order and derived criterion measures and where applicable the EPI Scales, were correlated with the degree class obtained by the sample of students in the Summer of 1974. These analyses were subsequently broken down by the sex and academic discipline of the students and the particular form of the 16PF.

Rather than reproduce all the data here, Tables 6.12 and 6.13 only give those correlation coefficients between degree class and the personality scales which differ significantly from zero at the five per cent and one per cent levels. Tables on the 16PF first order factors are given separately for the A/B and the C/D studies. The reader will also notice that scales which showed no statistically significant correlations have been omitted from the tables.

Table 6.12: Statistically significant correlations between 16PF first order factors and degree class Forms A and B

		B	F	G	H	I	L	M	N	O	Q3	Q4
Form A												
Females	Arts		−.15	.18								
	Science									−.20		
	Combined disciplines			.14[X]								
Males	Arts		−.18			−.19	.22x					
	Science							−.15				
	Combined disciplines						.15x					
Both Sexes	Arts	.10	−.16[X]	.12	−.13[X]		.14[X]					
	Science											
	Combined disciplines		−.09			.09	.12[X]					
Form B												
Females	Arts		−.14								.21[X]	−.14
	Science											−.20
	Combined disciplines		−.13			.10				.12	.16[X]	−.15[X]
Males	Arts		−.17									
	Science				−.16	.20[X]						
	Combined disciplines		−.13		−.13	.18[X]						
Both Sexes	Arts		−.16[X]		−.11	.12			.11			
	Science					.16[X]						
	Combined disciplines		−.13[X]		−.08	.15[X]						
Forms A+B												
Females	Arts		−.15								.18[X]	
	Science											
	Combined disciplines		−.12						.12		.13	
Males	Arts		−.19				.19					
	Science					.17						
	Combined disciplines		−.12			.15	.13					
Both Sexes	Arts	.12	−.17[X]		−.13							
	Science					.15						
	Combined disciplines		−.12[X]			.13[X]	.09					

All listed coefficients are significant at the 5% level.
Coefficients marked X are significant at the 1% level or beyond.

Table 6.13: Statistically significant correlations between 16PF first order factors and degree class Forms C and D

	B	C	E	F	I	L	M	Q1	Q2	Q3	Q4
Form C											
Females Arts					−.13	.14					
Science											
Combined disciplines		.13									
Males Arts					.18						
Science				−.19					.19		
Combined disciplines									.15^x		
Both Sexes Arts		.11	−.12		.13^x	−.11	.10				
Science											
Combined disciplines		.10	−.09								
Form D											
Females Arts	.14		−.16		.17^x						
Science		.22						.21			
Combined disciplines	.11	.12	−.10		.15^x						−.11
Males Arts											
Science									.16		
Combined disciplines									.11		
Both Sexes Arts	.11	.10	−.13^x		.12						−.10
Science		.13									
Combined disciplines	.11		−.09		.09					.09	−.14 / −.11^x
Forms C+D											
Females Arts	.15		−.16	.15							
Science		.22									
Combined disciplines		.15^x	−.11		.13^x						
Males Arts									.16		
Science				−.18					.18		
Combined disciplines			−.11						.16^x		
Both Sexes Arts	.13^x	.12	−.14^x	•	.14^x	.11					
Science		.12									
Combined disciplines		.12^x	−.10							.09	

All listed coefficients are significant at the 5% level.
Coefficients marked X are significant at the 1% level or beyond.

We are here dealing with statistical significance and not necessarily psychological or practical significance. The coefficients we report in Tables 6.12 and 6.13 are typically small, ranging from ±.09 to ±.22 and may or may not be of any value in practice. The practical worth of a correlation coefficient is very much to be judged on considerations in addition to its absolute size and statistical significance. If our aim is to predict degree class, these correlations are far from adequate. However, if we are more interested in testing psychological theories, even such small coefficients may be of importance, especially when one remembers that the reliability of degree class as a variable is probably only about .6 to .7. Moreover, because we are often dealing with personality scales of low reliability the degree of correlation will be attenuated still further. In fact, correcting the figures in Tables 6.12 and 6.13 for attentuation on both variables would mean that most of the co-efficients would fall between ±.15 and ±.35.

Perhaps the best way of dealing with the many correlation coefficients generated by the analysis is to summarize the statistically significant results and the general direction of the relationship by taking each factor in turn:

Factor A (Outgoing):
Zero
No significant relationships found with degree class either on the Forms A / B or Forms C / D studies.

Factor B (Intelligent):
Positive
Positively correlated in arts students in both studies.

Factor C (Emotionally Stable):
Positive
No relationships found on Forms A / B. Consistent relationships in Forms C / D, most noticeably in females.

Factor E (Dominant):
Negative
No relationship found in the Form A / B study. Some relationships in Forms C and D, mainly for arts students.

Factor F (Happy-go-Lucky):
Negative
A clear pattern in the Forms A / B study, being consistently related in arts students of both sexes. Little relationship in Forms C and D except in male science students.

Factor G (Conscientious):
Positive
Some positive relationship for arts students in Form A. No statistically significant findings in Form B or the Form C / D study.

Factor H (Socially Bold):
Negative
Significant negative coefficients, mainly in Form B. No relationship apparent in Forms C or D.

Factor I (Tender-Minded):
Positive
Related to degree class most strongly in Form B for male science students. Related in Forms C and D in arts students.

Factor L (Suspicious):
Negative
No clear pattern discernable; one significant relationship in male arts in Form A and in female arts students in Form C.

Factor M (Imaginative):
Positive
One significant correlation on Form A and in female arts students in Form C.

Factor N (Shrewd): Zero	One significant negative correlation in Form A and one significant positive correlation in Form B! No relationships in either Forms C or D.
Factor O (Guilt Prone): Zero	In Form A negatively correlated in female science students but positively correlated in Form B in arts students of combined sexes. No relationship found in Forms C or D.
Factor Q1 (Radical): Positive	Just one significant correlation found in female science students on Form D.
Factor Q2 (Self-sufficient): Positive	No findings on Form A and B but significant correlations for males on Forms C and D.
Factor Q3 (Controlled): *positive*	Significant relationships in female students on Form B and the total group of students on Form D.
Factor Q4 (Tense): Negative	No relationship on Form A but strong negative correlations for female students of both disciplines on Form B. No correlations on Form C but significant results on Form D with the combined discipline group of each sex.

It is reassuring that undergraduates tend to be higher in relation to young adults on those traits which are positively correlated with degree class and lower on those which are negatively correlated. The general direction of relationship between the personality scales and degree class has been indicated next to each of the factor names given above. These can be summarized as follows: Factor A zero, Factor B+, Factor C+, Factor E−, Factor F−, Factor G+, Factor H−, Factor I+, Factor L−, Factor M+, Factor N zero, Factor O zero, Factor Q1+, Factor Q2+, Factor Q3+ and Factor Q4−. These results are very much in line with the direction of differences between the undergraduate and young adult groups which we observed earlier.

Whether the universities and the other vehicles of selection are efficient at choosing individuals of the right characteristics for academic success or whether students project a particular personality favoured by the university environment is impossible to say but these results do suggest that some adaptive or perhaps self-fulfilling mechanisms are at work here.

The positive relationship of Factor I with degree class across both the studies is interesting in that Cattell and Butcher (1968) have suggested that high I, which they observed in academic researchers, may be an incidental and non-useful characteristic of academic selection. Clearly this is not borne out by this research. Not only are university students higher on this factor than young adults but those high on this trait are inclined to get better degrees.

Another finding which perhaps is of importance is the fact that Factor A shows no significant correlation with degree class in either of the two studies, whilst Factors F and H, as the two other major dimensions of Cattell's concept of Introversion / Extraversion (the second order factor of Exvia), do show significant relationships. This is further support for the argument that the 16PF successfully breaks down extraversion into meaningful and reliable sub-components.

Variation in results between forms of the 16PF is perhaps the most noticeable feature of these results. Bearing in mind the experimental design in which all students took Forms A and B or Forms C and D of the 16PF, we would expect that the factors which are significantly related to degree class on Form A for example, would show a similar relationship with degree class on Form B. Moreover, in view of the fact that allocating students the A / B or C / D questionnaires was carried out randomly, we would also expect high comparability between the two sets of results.

We can see from Table 6.12 that factors A,C,Q1 and Q2 on Forms A and B are consistent in the sense that they are not correlated with degree success in either form. But of the remaining ten factors only F, I, M and Q3 show patterns of correlations which are relatively stable across the two forms. The remaining Factors G, H, L, N, O and Q4 show the occasional correlation which reaches the five per cent level of significance but which is not replicated in the other form.

The same kind of inter-form variation is evident in the 16PF C / D results. Here Factors A, G, H, N, O are not significantly related to degree class on either form. Only Factors C and Q2 show a tolerably consistent relationship with degree class across forms, although B, E and I do relate with some regularity in arts students.

This all adds up to a rather confusing picture. Only Factor F— (the more Sober and Serious) across Forms A and B and Factors C+ and E— across Forms C and D (the more Emotionally Stable, but less Dominant) are reasonably consistently related to higher degree class. When results on the personality scales are compared across the two matched samples of students on Form A / B and Forms C / D, it is quite astonishing that if we take statistical significance as our criterion, there is no comparability of results whatsoever.

Thus, there would seem such a complex interplay of discipline, sex and form variation as to make any generalized statement on the relationship between the 16PF first order scales and degree class meaningless.

We are encouraged to speak not of 'Extraversion' but of 'Eysenck's Extraversion'. We can only conclude that such caution is perhaps not cautious enough; for it would seem that in relating academic attainment as measured by degree class with the 16PF first order personality scales, we need to prefix our description not only with Cattell's name but also the particular form of the 16PF in use.

Some may retort that we are unfair to these questionnaires and would point out that degree class is too unreliable a means by which to judge the personality scales. This has some truth. We would be foolish to concern ourselves unduly with the absolute size of the correlation. We have already noted above that, theoretically, the unreliability of the criterion (degree class) will restrict its relationship with other variables. However, when we are considering inter-form variation across the same sample of students, this point is not really relevant. Here any variation in results across Forms A and B, for example, must be due either to error in design of the study or to the personality scales under consideration. We have already noted that a counterbalanced scheme in questionnaire administration was adopted and so we are forced to conclude that most of the variation must lie in the vagaries of the scales themselves.

Where we are comparing the Forms A / B with the Forms C / D results, errors as a consequence of randomly assigning students across the two studies may be involved but it is by no means an invalid comparison. This is effectively what happens when we seek to reconcile the findings of investigators who have used different forms of the 16PF on different groups of students. They have the additional problem, moreover, that their student samples may not be as well matched or as large as they are here. It is small wonder then that so many conflicting conclusions are reached as to the rôle of certain personality characteristics in academic achievement.

Another potential criticism of our methodology is that we appear to be putting our results within the straitjacket of statistical significance. We should first remember, however, that on relatively large samples we are dealing with coefficients which may be far from having practical value and that statistical significance at the five per cent level may be the very least to be expected. The second defence to this point is that by including data on two form length in our summary tables, there is some safeguard against small inconsistencies in results between the forms.

16PF second orders, derived criteria and EPI correlations with degree class

The correlation of each of the 16PF second order factors and derived criteria with degree class are reproduced in Tables 6.14 and 6.15, where the EPI variables are also included. As with the first order correlations, only coefficients at the five per cent significance level or higher have been recorded and scales have been omitted from the tables where no significant results were found.

The first comments we can make regarding these tables is that the separate coefficients are relatively low (the highest is in fact .23) and that they show considerable form variation. Let us consider the scales in order:

Exvia: Negative	Significant negative correlations mainly in Form B arts students.
Anxiety:	No findings in the forms A / B study but one negative correlation in Form D which just reaches statistical significance.
Prodigal Subjectivity: Positive	Some positive correlation with degree class, mainly in forms A and B.
Intelligence: Positive	This second order factor is almost totally the first order factor B scale and shows an almost identical pattern of correlations.
Super-Ego Strength: Positive	Some positive relationships in both studies, mainly in arts students.
Tough Poise: Negative	This factor is negatively correlated with degree success in Forms A, B and C, for arts students of both sexes.
Independence: Zero	No significant findings across any of the groups or forms.
Discreetness:	One positive coefficient in Form B for female students which just reaches significance.

The negative correlations of Exvia with degree class is not altogether surprising, as extraversion as measured by various scales and questionnaires has been shown to be negatively related to academic achievement in numerous studies (Entwistle, 1972). The role of anxiety is also interesting, if more confused. In these studies we find only one small negative correlation whereas in the literature there have been suggestions that both those of high and low anxiety are at risk academically (Derrick, 1971).

We may reasonably suspect therefore that the relationship may be curvilinear in the form of an inverted 'U', such that those very high and those very low on anxiety perform worst in terms of degree class. Were this the case, the general linear model, which is implicit in most of our analyses, would not fit and the effect would be overlooked. To test this possibility, scores on 16PF Forms A + B and C + D Anxiety and EPI Neuroticism were divided into three ranges corresponding to high, medium and low anxiety and contingency tables prepared for anxiety / neuroticism by degree class and by sex and discipline. The results of this analysis were inconclusive; two chi-squares just reached significance at the .05 level but in neither case could the hypotheses be said to be supported. Nevertheless, this does not rule out the possibility of non-linear relationships between degree class and personality. Much academic failure will have taken place before the students' second year and for this reason our data are not well suited to testing this theory.

The third second order factor Cortertia, or more popularly Tough Poise, is an abbreviation by Cattell for 'cortical alertness'. Our results suggest therefore that those arts students who are of lower cortical arousal and operate at a mood level rather than handle problems

Table 6.14: Statistically significant correlations between 16PF second order factors and degree class Forms A and B

		Exvia	Cortertia	Discreetness	Prodigal subjectivity	Intelligence	Superego strength	Neuroticism	Leadership	Creativity	School achievement
	Form A										
Females	Arts						.15				.20[X]
	Science										
	Combined disciplines						.11				.16[X]
Males	Arts				.18				−.17		.19
	Science									.21[X]	
	Combined disciplines				.16[X]					.18[X]	.15
Both Sexes	Arts	−.13	−.12			.11	.11				
	Science										
	Combined disciplines										
	Form B										
Females	Arts	−.18[X]								.13	
	Science										
	Combined disciplines	−.12		.11			.11			.12	.11
Males	Arts							.19	−.18		
	Science									.20	
	Combined disciplines	−.12	−.14					.13	−.12	.16[X]	
Both Sexes	Arts	−.16[X]	−.15								
	Science				.13						
	Combined disciplines	−.11[X]	−.13[X]		.10						
	Forms A+B										
Females	Arts	−.15					.16[X]				.18[X]
	Science										
	Combined disciplines			.10			.12			.10	.15[X]
Males	Arts				.19			.17	−.17		.18
	Science									.23[X]	
	Combined disciplines				.15[X]					.19[X]	.14
Both Sexes	Arts	−.15[X]	−.14[X]			.11					
	Science				.13						
	Combined disciplines	−.09	−.10		.10						

All listed coefficients are significant at the 5% level.
Coefficients marked X are significant at the 1% level or beyond.

Table 6.15: Statistically significant correlations between 16PF (Forms C and D) second order factors, EPI—E and degree class

		Exvia	Anxiety	Cortertia	Prodigal subjectivity	Intelligence	Super ego strength	Creativity	School achievement	EPI E
Form C										
Females	Arts			−.17^x				.15		−.15
	Science									
	Combined disciplines			−.11						
Males	Arts									
	Science	−.16								
	Combined disciplines							.14	.13	−.15
Both Sexes	Arts			−.12	.10					
	Science									
	Combined disciplines									
Form D										
Females	Arts					.16		.18^x		
	Science									
	Combined disciplines				.12	.14^x		.14^x		
Males	Arts									
	Science									
	Combined disciplines						.11	.13	.13	
Both Sexes	Arts					.13^x	.11			
	Science									
	Combined disciplines		−.09				.09			
Forms C+D										
Females	Arts									
	Science									
	Combined disciplines							.12		
Males	Arts									
	Science	−.17					:16		.16	
	Combined disciplines	−.11					.11	.16^x	.17^x	
Both Sexes	Arts			−.13^x	.11	.14^x				
	Science									
	Combined disciplines						.08			

All listed coefficients are significant at the 5% level.
Coefficients marked X are significant at the 1% level or beyond.

objectively, tend to gain better degrees! It could be argued however that the sizeable positive correlation which Cortertia has with Exvia, especially for females, is not unconnected here.

The general findings on Cattell's derived criteria measures are as follows:

Neuroticism: Positive	Significant correlation in male arts students on Form B. No relationship in Forms C or D.
Leadership: Negative	This derived criterion measure shows negative correlations with degree class in male arts students in Form A and Form B. No significant findings in Forms C or D.
Creativity: Positive	Significant positive correlations across all forms for the two disciplines and both sexes.
School Achievement: Positive	Related to degree class in arts students on Forms A and B when the sexes are taken separately. Some statistically significant correlations on Forms C and D also.

The positive correlation between the Neuroticism derived criterion (Form B) and degree class of male arts students would seem to go against our findings on the second order Anxiety factor, where zero order coefficients were the rule and, in fact, there is one negative correlation in Form D.

As we have observed in an earlier section, Neuroticism tends to have a high negative correlation with Exvia (about $-.6$). Indeed, Cattell's Neurotics can be said to be neurotic introverts in Eysenck's terminology and, therefore, it could be the high saturation of Neuroticism with the introversion factor which is responsible for these apparently conflicting results.

In general, just as Cattell's neurotics are Eysenck's unstable-introverts, then Cattell's leaders are Eysenck's stable-extraverts. It is not totally surprising, then, that the Leadership derived criterion shows negative correlations with degree class in various groups. Another interpretation, of course, is that there is some tendency for those who gain better university degrees to be poor leaders!

The two remaining derived criteria both show consistent positive relationships with degree class; Creativity, with the first order factors of Reservedness (A−), Intelligence (B+) and Tender-Mindedness (I+) as its major components and School Achievement, with Intelligence (B+), Conscientiousness (G+) and Self-sufficiency (Q2+) all loading highly.

To summarize the results on the Eysenck Personality Inventory:

EPI Extraversion: Negative	Significant negative correlations with degree class in female arts students and male combined discipline students.
EPI Neuroticism: Zero	No statistically significant correlations found.
EPI Lie Scale: Zero	No statistically significant correlations found.

On the EPI scales the two negative correlations of Extraversion re-confirms our earlier observations on the role of this personality factor in degree performance. However, most of the correlations were not significant in the majority of groups studied.

Multiple regression analyses

The presentation of tables of correlations between 16PF scale scores and the criterion of degree class once more raises the question of the extent to which the relationships may be exaggerated by scale intercorrelations. A technique for coping with this problem is, of course, at hand in the form of multiple regression analysis. Essentially, this yields a set of weights to be applied to scale scores to produce a composite score, which has the maximum possible correlation with the criterion.

The particular method we have adopted is the stepwise multiple regression technique as implemented in version 5 of the Statistical Package for the Social Sciences (Nie, Bent and Hall, 1970). This proceeds by first choosing the single variable which is the best predictor of the criterion; the second independent variable to be added to the regression equation is that which provides the best prediction in conjunction with the first. Variables are thus added successively until no other variable will make a significant contribution to the prediction equation.

Table 6.16 gives the multiple correlation of the 16PF first order factors and the EPI for diverse form variations on student groups divided by sex and discipline. The figure provided in parenthesis in each cell of the table represents the number of variables entered into the multiple regression equations. Four different form combinations in each study were used as a basis for these equations. The first two combinations are where each form is taken separately, the third where all 32 first order variables across both forms are used and the fourth combination involved the summation of the raw scores on the same factors across the two forms to give 16 first order factor scores based on two form length. Of course, the multiple correlations listed in the table are based on the assumption of a linear relationship between the predictor (personality) and predicted (degree class) variables.

It can be seen from Table 6.16 that the multiple correlation

Table 6.16: Multiple correlation of the Personality Scales with degree class

Group		N	16PF Forms A / B Study				N	16PF Forms C / D Study				EPI
			Form A	Form B	Forms A&B	Forms A+B		Form C	Form D	Forms C&D	Forms C+D	
Females	Arts	221	.33* (14)	.42* (16)	.48* (31)	.34* (15)	218	.35* (16)	.28 (16)	.43* (30)	.33* (16)	.15 (2)
	Science	115	.33 (15)	.40 (15)	.56* (30)	.30 (14)	112	.28 (13)	.39 (14)	.46* (27)	.37 (15)	.21 (2)
	Combined disciplines	336	.25 (16)	.35* (15)	.41* (30)	.27* (16)	330	.26 (15)	.28* (16)	.37* (31)	.28* (16)	.09 (2)
Males	Arts	131	.45* (14)	.36 (13)	.51* (32)	.42 (14)	138	.32 (15)	.26 (15)	.41 (29)	.30 (14)	.19 (2)
	Science	143	.33 (15)	.46* (14)	.54* (29)	.39 (15)	143	.35 (14)	.33 (15)	.43 (28)	.37 (16)	.15 (2)
	Combined disciplines	274	.31 (14)	.32* (15)	.43* (31)	.31 (15)	281	.25 (12)	.22 (13)	.29 (30)	.26 (15)	.16* (2)
Both Sexes	Arts	352	.34* (16)	.33* (15)	.41* (28)	.31* (15)	356	.30* (16)	.22 (14)	.37* (32)	.28* (16)	.16* (2)
	Science	250	.21 (16)	.28 (15)	.34* (28)	.25 (12)	255	.23 (16)	.28 (13)	.33* (30)	.26 (14)	.10 (2)
	Combined disciplines	610	.24* (16)	.28* (16)	.34* (30)	.25* (16)	611	.22* (14)	.22* (15)	.28* (31)	.23* (16)	.12* (2)

* Significant at the 5% level or beyond

coefficients range from .21 to .56 with the majority in the .3's and .4's and about 50 per cent significant at the .05 level or beyond. Note that either Forms A or B on their own seem better predictors than either Forms C or D, where the multiple correlations with degree class are not high and usually not statistically significant. Moreover, there may well be some tendency for Form B to be a better predictor of degree class than Form A. It can also be seen that Forms C + D (i.e. where factors have been summed across the two forms giving 16 variables in all) is about as good predictively as either Forms A or B of the 16PF on its own.

When we consider the effect of summing factors across Forms of the 16PF, rather than keeping them separate in the analyses (i.e. dealing with 16 as against 32 variables), it would seem that some degree of predictive accuracy is lost. This would not be the case if the forms were truly comparable. We should be cautious on this point, however, especially when dealing with small groups where there will be a greater tendency for 32 variables to capitalize on chance effects and so produce higher multiple correlation coefficients.

Since multiple regression tends to capitalize on chance effects in the data, the application of regression weights derived from one sample to scores for another, will result in shrinkage in these multiple correlations. Moreover, use of a different form of a test may cause even greater shrinkage. In particular, given the inter-form variation we have had occasion to discuss elsewhere, this will undoubtedly apply to alternate forms of the 16PF. The generalized regression equations provided by Cattell (1970) to predict behavioural criteria will clearly be prone to this effect. However, since a relatively large number of variables (i.e. 16) are typically entered into the regression equation, their number and intercorrelation will help to counteract this tendency. That is to say, as there is variance in common between the scales of the 16PF, there are many possible sets of regression weights which would be equally valid.

From Table 6.16 it would appear that the degree class of arts students is better predicted than that of science students. Similarly, despite our initial prejudices to the contrary, females would seem more predictable than males! Although we must bear in mind chance effects mentioned above, Seashore (1962) and Gross *et al*. (1974) have observed the tendency in other psychometric data. The prime influence here certainly appears to be with the female arts students, who are the single most predictable group in terms of degree class.

In the light of our previous discussion on the comparability of the Eysenck and Cattell scales, it is perhaps relevant to ask whether the EPI factors provide multiple correlations with degree class of the same order as those of the 16PF. Table 6.16 shows that in three cases significant multiple correlations between EPI scales and degree class are to be found but generally this is where 16PF scales also yield a significant result. However, in these three cases the EPI multiple correlations are lower in absolute terms than 16PF multiple correlations. Of course, with 16 scales the 16PF is more likely to capitalize on chance effects in the data but it is possible to undertake a statistical F test to determine the extent to which 16PF has benefited unfairly in the comparison. The results of this test suggest that in fact there is very little to choose between Forms C and D of the 16PF and the EPI.

It does occur to us, however, that the results of this analysis very much depend on the particular technique of multiple regression employed and the number of variables entered in the multiple regression equation. Unfortunately, it is the indeterminacy associated with multiple correlation methods which makes interpretation very difficult. The choice of a stepwise method, and of a particular criterion for entering a variable into the equation, is essentially arbitrary. Where the intercorrelations of predictor variables are substantial, the number of possible sets of regression coefficients is indefinitely large, such that results are entirely dependent on the particular procedure adopted.

With our method the first three or four variables entered have the maximum effect on the multiple R and adding further variables on the one hand adds little to the size of the correlation but, on the other, reduces the degrees of freedom upon which the significance test is based. With more variables then, one needs a higher coefficient in order to reach significance. As a practical example on this point, whilst on the male arts students group, entering 32 variables for the 16PF Forms A and B produces a multiple R of .51, the first four variables alone gave a value of .40. The judgement as to whether the 16PF is statistically superior to the EPI in terms of predicting degree class will rest in part, therefore, on precisely at what stage the multiple regression analysis is terminated.

For these reasons, it is very difficult to draw hard and fast conclusions on the relative efficacy of the two questionnaires. The 16PF and EPI are both far from adequate devices if our goal is the individual prediction of degree success. If our aim on the other hand, is an understanding of the role of personality in academic achievement, despite the inconsistencies the 16PF may well be of value in describing variables which operate in addition to Eysenck's two-factor theory. We have already noticed, for example, the importance of Factors such as I and B in our bivariate analysis.

The apparent inconsistencies of these personality scales in predicting degree class could lead one to doubt the value of introducing personality traits as intervening variables in predicting behavioural outcomes. Are mediating variables really the simplest answer? Many personality test items are clearly relevant to the kind of behaviour which at a commonsense level would seem to be related to academic success. Some introversion scales, for example, contain items such as 'Do you prefer to read a book or go to a party?' It is not altogether surprising that scales containing such items turn out to be related to final degree class. The essential point though is whether it is necessary to introduce a concept like introversion to explain this phenomenon. One must beware of falling into the error of assuming that correlational relationships between a hypothetical construct and criterion imply causal mechanisms and that such a relationship as we have found is direct evidence for the objective existence of the construct.

This could lead one to the view, almost blasphemous in the present context, that perhaps the development of special-purpose instruments has more potential for empirical prediction of scholastic attainment. All the same, general-purpose instruments seem to be of rather limited practical value and. where any statistically significant findings emerge, they could well be as a result of a small number of relevant items tapping relatively specific behaviours. Even custom built tests, however, have their drawbacks, not least of which is their lack of sensitivity in different situations.

Summary

We began this chapter with a comparison between our undergraduate samples and a group of British young adults of corresponding age. Despite the unreliability of some 16PF scales there were clear differences between these groups with the undergraduates, in Cattell's terms, being more radical, introverted and tenderminded. The two main discriminators between the groups, however, were the 16PF Intelligence Scale (B) and the factor named by Cattell as Imagination or Inner Mental Life (M). When we came to the correlational study relating the degree class of the follow-up sample with the personality scales in question, there was a general picture emerging of Conscientiousness, Intelligence, Tendermindedness and Emotional Stability being positively related to achievement.

Against these findings we must remember that most of the differences in means are relatively small and indeed the correlations of degree class are typically low. Often a 16PF factor is inconsistent across forms on the same sub-group and although multiple correlation between the 16PF personality scales and degree class are generally about .4 to .5, the multiple correlation approach is known to capitalize on chance with the result that coefficients corrected for shrinkage will be lower than these values.

On the other hand it should not be forgotten that the criterion (degree class) is a conglomerate variable. We have not sought to measure study methods and interests which almost certainly play a part in academic achievement. There is also the point that the criterion is unreliable and probably shows different distributions in the various academic subjects. If we are interested in theory rather than pure statistical prediction, we must also bear in mind that our predictors similarly lack reliability. Despite this however, it must be said that some scales, for example Factor C in the A / B study, show correlations about as high as those obtained with the ability test used by Choppin *et al.* (1973).

Another relevant issue is the point that we have only investigated the relationship between degree class and personality on a linear model. Nevertheless there can be structure in data without linearity. Entwistle (1974) has shown using a cluster analysis computer program that whilst certain variables such as study methods and motivation generally show simple relationships to degree class, Extraversion and Neuroticism as measured by the EPI act in more complex and contradictory ways in combining with other variables. For example, two distinct groups in his sample of students receiving a high degree class were stable students of high motivation and neurotic introverts of low motivation.

The possibility of discovering a typology of student types who gain a high degree class is very attractive but alas similar problems exist with cluster analysis as with factor analysis. There are the problems of deciding what constitutes a cluster and the fact that there are a great many different cluster analysis procedures means that the cluster solutions will vary depending upon the program used. Moreover, there are chance effects in cluster analysis as in any statistical procedure and the vital question is whether cluster analysis provides any better prediction on cross-validation than the multiple regression approach. In addition cluster analysis is a relatively recent innovation and tends to be very consuming of computer resources. It is nevertheless an approach which deserves to be investigated more fully in the future.

Chapter 7

Summary and Conclusions

As we turn now to a summary of the findings, it is perhaps as well to recapitulate the original aims and purpose of the survey. Essentially we are concerned with two modes of inquiry: the study of the British undergraduate in terms of some of the most commonly used personality tests, and the study of the tests themselves in the light of the data provided by our sample. The reader will recall that the sample (N = 2584) consists entirely of undergraduates in their second year of study at British universities; that the administration of the questionnaires was arranged so as to eliminate as far as possible situational biases; and that in point of fact the robustness of the sample has been apparent in the relatively close comparability of the parameters of our sample with official statistics.

Conclusions concerning the students

1. There were differences in personality between the sexes which were closely in line with those found in general population adults. On the 16PF first order factors 13 of the factors showed statistically significant differences. There was a general picture emerging of females being more Emotionally Labile (C−, O+, Q4+), Tender-minded (I+) and less Dominant (E−) than male students. As with any statistical analysis based on large sample sizes, some of these differences rested on relatively small differences in means.

2. When the student groups were classified by academic discipline, clear personality differences emerged. There was an interaction with sex variation here, with arts students higher on anxiety components and perhaps on extraversion. As with the sex differences, the major discriminator was on the 16PF Tender-mindedness (I) scale with arts students of both sexes being considerably higher than science undergraduates. Unlike findings

on earlier studies, there was no clear pattern of differences between the disciplines in intelligence, perhaps because of the verbal bias of the 16PF intelligence scale. In general our data support the hypothesis that those students following 'people' orientated areas of study (arts subjects) are more anxious / neurotic, tenderminded and radical than those following practical or 'thing' orientated courses.

3. When a comparison was made between the results based on British undergraduates and the norm tables prepared by Cattell on American students, the British undergraduate was seen as more Introverted (A−,F−,H−), Experimenting (Q1+), Intelligent (B+), Imaginative (M+) and Self-sufficient (Q2+). Caution was sounded, however, on interpreting the differences in Factor B of the 16PF as a result of the far more stringent selection undertaken in British universities.

4. With regard to the comparison between university undergraduates and young adults of a comparable age, it was found that undergraduates tended to be more Intelligent (B+), Imaginative (M+), Tender-minded (I+), Self-sufficient (Q2+) and Introverted (Exvia −). They were also, perhaps, rather more emotionally stable (C+,Q4−). This goes against some previous research which found students to be higher on anxiety. It was suggested that the nature of the scales used, the characteristics of the criterion samples and the time and conditions of testing, may all be relevant here.

5. Approximately 1400 students were followed up from their second to third years and their degree class correlated with the personality scales. A good deal of discipline, sex and form variation was noted but, despite inconsistencies, evidence was found that on the 16PF students gaining better degrees tended to be more Intelligent (B+), Emotionally Stable (C+), Conscientious (G+), Imaginative (M+), Experimenting (Q1+), Self-sufficient (Q2+), Controlled (Q3+) and Tender-minded (I+). They were also less Dominant (E−), Happy-go-Lucky (F−), Socially-Bold (H−), Suspicious (L−) and Tense (Q4−). Cattell's derived criteria of School Achievement and Creativity were also related to degree class. In general it was found that the scales which were significantly correlated with degree class were the same personality factors which discriminated under-graduates from young adults.

6. When the degree analysis was broken down by the sex and academic discipline of the students, female arts undergraduates were found to be the most predictable on the linear model. It would seem, therefore, that the finding on cognitive tests that females are more predictable than males may also apply to personality data.

7. Although there was a general tendency for introverted students to gain better degrees, the results suggest that it is only certain of Cattell's first order introversion factors which are related to degree class. It may be that it is not introversion but perhaps a particular kind of introversion which is involved in academic achievement.

8. The theory that anxiety shows a curvilinear relationship to degree class was investigated but no consistent results were found. It was pointed out, however, that the study was not principally designed to research such relationships.

9. In all, the results demonstrate very great difficulties in making generalized statements about the personality of university students. Although sex differences are to be found which are very much in line with those in general population adults, there appear to be deep-rooted personality differences between the academic disciplines which must also be taken into account. Moreover, if results are to be replicated, great care should be taken to specify the scales being used.

Conclusions concerning the scales

1. The 16PF alternate form reliability coefficients calculated on British university students tended to be as high or higher than those reported by Cattell. Nevertheless, the reliabilities on certain first order factors are very low and make profile interpretation of the primaries extremely hazardous.

2. There is a very considerable inter-form variation in the direction and size of inter-group differences, such that to specify differences in terms of 'Cattell's Factor N', for instance, rather than '16PF Form A Factor N', may be to invite immediate contradiction by those using another form of the test.

3. Furthermore, although in certain instances reliability coefficients are respectably high, for some scales correlations with other factors on the same or a different form are as high as the reliability of those scales. In particular this is so for the three major first order 'Anxiety' factors, *viz*. Factors C, O, Q4.

4. This inter-form variation may be thought to account for the vanishingly small increment in multiple correlations with degree class obtained by summing scale scores on alternate forms. It would seem that at least for the purposes of multiple regression, 16PF 'alternate' forms should be treated as independent.

5. Notwithstanding this variability, there are a number of inter-group differences which are consistently related to certain of Cattell's scales across all forms, such that the reader should not conclude from the above strictures that such differences will always be a matter of chance. Against the suggestion that Cattell's factor

structure is entirely inappropriate, there is the possibility that the scaling characteristics of the various factors on the various forms are different and that further development work is needed to perfect the scales.

6. Certain factors for which there was no clear equivalent in the EPI were related to degree class, though results tended to be inconsistent across forms of the 16PF. Generally, multiple correlations, even when corrected for shrinkage, tended to be higher for the 16PF primaries than for the EPI but the difficulties of a generalized multiple regression equation were pointed out.

7. A high correspondence was found between Eysenck's Extraversion and Neuroticism scales and the Exvia and Anxiety second order factors of Cattell's 16PF.

8. Although Cattell has argued that neuroticism is different from anxiety in that it is a pathological disorder of which anxiety is just one symptom, from these analyses Cattell's Neuroticism derived criterion could simply be described as an amalgam of anxiety and introversion.

9. In comparison with the Eysenck Personality Inventory, Cattell's 16PF covers more ground. Since Eysenck does not claim to measure various of the traits appearing in the 16PF, namely Factors B (Intelligence), I (Tough-mindedness) and Q2 (Radicalism), the disagreement on these scales remains centred on their reliability. There can be no doubt however that these scales were found to be important and efficient discriminators between various of the groups studied here.

10. It would appear that Cattell has successfully split down extraversion into more than one component factor. When the EPI *E* was extracted from the 16PF, Factors A (Outgoing), E (Assertive), H (Venturesome) and Q2 (Group-dependence) still appeared as relatively strong factors.

11. The same cannot be said for the anxiety dimension since the three important 16PF first order Anxiety scales, Factors C, O and Q4, have to all intents and purposes equal reliabilities and inter-correlations. When the EPI *N* scale was extracted much of the variance on these particular 16PF factors was exhausted. Moreover, these scales all tended to behave in consistent directions with regard to group differences.

12. Even after extraction of a five factor model of personality (Eysenck's *E* and *N* plus the 16PF Factors B, I and Q2), Cattell's Factor G, named Super-ego Strength, remained as an important and relatively reliable factor.

13. On our undergraduate samples only a moderate correlation was found between Cattell's Motivational Distortion (MD) and Eysenck

Lie scales.

14. Of course, the recent introduction of the Eysenck Personality Questionnaire (1976), based on a three dimensional model of personality of Extraversion, Introversion and the variable of Psychoticism, which Eysenck has popularly labelled 'Tough-mindedness', may erode still further the 16PF variance left unaccounted for by the EPI, more particularly with regard to Cattell's Factor I and possibly G (Super-ego Strength).

15. Finally, we shall summarize our results on the 16PF first order factors, for it is here that controversy is rife. In describing the findings on the alternate form reliability of the 16PF, we shall adopt a more contemporary 'soft' line to reliability theory.

16PF Factor A (Reserved v Outgoing): This factor was shown to be a relatively reliable component of Cattell's second order factor Exvia. However, it was not well covered by the EPI *E* Scale and seems to work relatively independently of Cattell's other first order measures of introversion. As with British adults, female university students tend to score above their male counterparts on this factor. It is also a scale which discriminates between academic disciplines with arts students significantly higher than science undergraduates. In addition Factor A shows clear differences, in females at least, between the undergraduate and young adult samples. This primary showed no statistically significant relationship with degree class despite the significant correlations which other of Cattell's introversion factors demonstrated. In all, this scale would appear a relevant and reliable sub-factor of the introversion / extraversion factor found in various questionnaires.

16PF Factor B (Less intelligent v More intelligent): Cattell's measure of intelligence was shown to be rather unreliable, especially in this restricted population. However, as expected, what reliable variance it possessed seemed independent of that in the EPI and it was found to be an important discriminator between undergraduates and young adults. In certain analyses this factor was also relevant to degree class.

This is perhaps an example of an unreliable scale measuring a distinguishable questionnaire factor. Despite this unreliability there can be no doubt that in view of the length of the scale and the lack of control on timing, Factor B can be a useful dimension, particularly when dealing with group differences. It is unlikely, on the other hand, to be satisfactory for the assessment of individuals, especially at the university level.

16PF Factor C (Affected by feelings v Emotionally stable): This is a relatively reliable factor but showed a very high correlation with

Factors O (Guilt-Prone) and Q4 (Tense), which are Cattell's two other primary measures of anxiety. Indeed, these correlations were so considerable as to make it virtually impossible to distinguish this factor as a separate identity. The scale was well covered by Eysenck's Neuroticism Scale in the EPI. With regard to sex differences, males generally exceed females on this factor and there is also some evidence that science students score higher than arts undergraduates. Moreover, the student group scored significantly above the young adult sample. It is also interesting to note that the direction of these differences are generally in line with those we would expect on Factors O and Q4. This factor showed positive relationship with degree class in certain forms of the 16PF.

16PF Factor E (Humble v Assertive): This was another factor of relatively good reliability which showed unique variance when the two EPI factors were extracted. In the undergraduate sample, male scores tended to surpass females' for every 16PF form combination. There were no clear discipline differences on this factor nor were the differences significant between the student and the young adult samples. With regard to degree class, no relationships were found in the 16PF Forms A and B study but some significant negative correlations were found in Forms C and D.

16PF Factor F (Sober v Happy-go-lucky): A sub-factor of Cattell's Exvia, this primary was found to be of reasonable reliability but most of its variance was adequately covered by the EPI. This factor seems closer to Eysenck's concept of Extraversion than Factor A dealt with above. No consistent sex nor academic discipline differences were found but young adults tended to be significantly higher than undergraduates. Some negative relationships were found between this scale and degree class.

16PF Factor G (Expedient v Conscientious): Reliabilities were relatively high on this factor and it was not one well covered by the EPI. There may be some tendency for females to score higher but no clear discipline differences emerged. Similarly, it did not discriminate between young adults and undergraduates. There was some positive relationship between this factor and degree class for arts students on Form A of the 16PF but not for the other forms used in the study.

16PF Factor H (Shy v Venturesome): This was the most reliable first order factor of the 16PF; as reliable in fact as the first two of Cattell's second order factors. Some variance was still left after extraction of the two EPI scales by the arbitrary factoring technique and some significant negative correlations with degree class were found. Sex differences on this factor seemed to rest on the particular forms of the 16PF in use but discipline differences, in males at least, were found with male arts scoring higher than male science students.

16PF Factor I (Tough-minded v Tender-minded): Reasonably adequate in terms of reliability, this factor was probably the most susceptible to group differences. Invariably male groups scored lower than female, there usually being about one standard deviation unit between the sexes. Very large differences were found, moreover, between academic disciplines, with arts undergraduates scoring significantly more highly than science students. There was clear discrimination on Factor I between the young adults and student groups and there was also a tendency for positive relationship with degree class. After extraction of the EPI two-factor model, variance still remained in this scale. However, further studies should seek the relationship between this factor and Eysenck's Psychoticism which may be a close equivalent. Judging from item-content, it is also possible that Factor I is a measure of masculine / non-aesthetic versus feminine / aesthetic interests as much as 'Tender-mindedness.'

16PF Factor L (Trusting v Suspicious): This is a relatively unreliable factor but despite this there is unique variance left after extraction of the EPI. Male scores tend to be higher than female scores on this factor but there are no consistent differences with regard to academic discipline. Although there was no clear pattern when this factor was related to degree class, undergraduates tend to score higher than their peers in the general population. In view of all the evidence which we have before us, it is difficult to weigh up the importance of this particular factor. This could be another example of a factor with some claim for existence but which is poorly measured by the current 16PF personality test items. On the other hand, this scale conceivably could be measuring some form of response set.

16PF Factor M (Practical v Imaginative): This particular factor was a major discriminator between the student and young adult samples and shows some overlap with Cattell's first order of Intelligence (Factor B). Factor M was found to be relatively unreliable in the student sample and the cause of this does not seem to be in any tendency for students' scores to be restricted in range. There is no discernable pattern of sex differences on this factor although evidence was found of arts students scoring higher than science students. Some evidence was found of a positive relationship on this scale with degree class. Whilst the EPI did not account for much of this factor, there was relatively little reliable variance remaining after extraction of the 16PF Factor B (Intelligence).

16PF Factor N (Forthright v Shrewd): This was the most unreliable of all of Cattell's first order factors (in the Forms C and D study reliabilities were down to 0.1). There were no apparent discipline differences although there may be a tendency for female scores to surpass males'. When the EPI variables were extracted from this 16PF primary, nearly all reliable variance was lost, mainly as a result of its high correlation with Eysenck's Extraversion. Young adults were found to be higher on this factor but of the two significant correlations with degree class, one was negative and one positive. There would seem to be very little evidence that Factor N in any way constitutes a reliable personality variable.

16PF Factor O (Self-assured v Apprehensive): This is a factor of reasonable reliability and one on which females are usually higher than males. Moreover, in Forms C and D at least, arts score higher than science students. In relation to degree class both significant positive and negative correlations were found. This factor, as we noted before, has high correlation with Factor C (Emotionally Stable) and Factor Q4 (Tense) and its own reliabilities are about as high as its intercorrelations with these factors. There was very little reliable variance left after the EPI two-factor model had been extracted. It would seem therefore that Factor O is probably the result of an arbitrary splitting of the anxiety component in the 16PF.

16PF Factor Q1 (Conservative v Experimenting): Generally males are higher than females on this factor and arts students higher than science undergraduates. The scale also acted as a discriminator between the student and young adult sample. Despite only modest reliability, a good deal of variance remained after extraction of the EPI Scales and for this reason Factor Q1 was used as a target vector in our arbitrary factoring. This may be an important personality variable and, indeed, it is one which appears to have a close analogue, for example, in Eysenck's theory of social attitudes.

16PF Factor Q2 (Group dependent v Self-sufficient): Although by no means consistent, males are generally higher than females on this factor but there appears to be no stable pattern of differences between the disciplines. Undergraduates were significantly higher than young adults here and in the Form C and D study at least, the scale was positively correlated with degree class. Alternate form reliabilities could only be described as moderate on this factor but nevertheless unique variance remained even after extraction of the five factor model of personality.

It should be pointed out, however, that Factor Q2 shows some negative correlation with Factor A (Out-going) and it is not impossible that they are sharing a pool of common variance.

16PF Factor Q3 (Undisciplined self-conflict v Controlled): In general males are higher than female undergraduates and the same is true of science over arts students. Reliability is relatively satisfactory and this factor did show some positive correlation with degree class. Unique variance remained after extraction of both the two and five factor models of personality but sizeable correlations were reported between this factor and the 16PF Factor G (Conscientious).

16PF Factor Q4 (Relaxed v Tense): Another of Cattell's anxiety components in the 16PF, this factor was reasonably reliable but showed very high correlations with Factors C (Emotionally-Stable) and O (Guilt-Prone). Males tended to score lower than females and undergraduates lower than young adults. Significant negative correlations were found with degree class. After extraction of the EPI Neuroticism Scale, very little reliable variance remained in this scale. It is difficult to see this scale as being in any way separate to the other anxiety components of the 16PF.

Whereas then, Cattell's personality scales appear to be more comprehensive in coverage than those of Eysenck, it does not seem that the 16PF primary factors are necessarily the simplest or best solution. We shall resist the temptation to offer any alternative formulations at this point but from these studies on undergraduates perhaps a seven or eight factor solution would suffice to contain most of the reliable variance to be found in the questionnaires. This is not to say, of course, that other important personality variables do not exist but rather, in our student samples, they were difficult to distinguish as reliable, separate identities.

REFERENCES

ADCOCK, C.J. (1965) 'A comparison of the concepts of Cattell and Eysenck: research notes,' *British Journal of Educational Psychology* 35, 90—7.

ALLMAN, T.W. and WHITE, W.F. (1968) 'Birth order categories as predictors of select personality characteristics,' *Psychological Reports,* 22, 857—60.

ANASTASI, A. (1961) *Psychological Testing.* 2nd Edition. New York: Macmillan Co.

ARNHOFF, F.N. and LEON, H.V. (1963) 'Personality factors related to success and failure in sensory deprivation subjects,' *Perceptual and Motor Skills*, 16, 46.

BAKKER, C.B. and LEVENSON, R.M. (1967) 'Determinants of angina pectoris,' *Psychosomatic Medicine*, 29, 621—33.

BAREFOOT, J.C. (1969) 'Anxiety and volunteering,' *Psychonomic Science*, 16(6), 283—4.

BARTON, K. and CATTELL, R.B. (1972) 'Personality factors related to job promotion and turnover,' *Journal of Counselling Psychology*, 19, 5, 430—35.

BARTON, K., DIELMAN, T.E. and CATTELL, R.B. (1972) 'Personality, motivation and IQ measures as predictors of school achievement and grades — a non-technical synopsis,' *Psychology in the Schools*, 9, 1.

BECKER, W.C. (1960) 'The matching of behaviour rating and questionnaire personality factors,' *Psychological Bulletin*, 57, 3.

BECKER, W.C. (1961) 'A comparison of the factor structure and other properties of the 16PF and the Guilford-Martin Personality Inventories,' *Educational and Psychological Measurement*, XXI, 2.

BOORER, D. and MURGATROYD, S. (1973) *Personality and Learning — a select annotated bibliography.* Caerphilly: MTM Publishing House (Wales).

BROWNE, M.W. (1972) 'Oblique rotation to a partially specified target,' *British Journal of Mathematical and Statistical Psychology*, 25, 207—12.

BROWNE, M.W. (1972) 'Orthogonal rotation to a partially specified target,' *British Journal of Mathematical and Statistical Psychology*, 25, 115—20.

BROWNE, M. and KRISTOF, W. (1969) 'On the oblique rotation of a factor matrix to a specified pattern,' *Psychometrika*, 34, 2.

BUROS, O.K. (Editor) (1972) *The Seventh Mental Measurements Yearbook* (Vols I and II). Highland Park, New Jersey, USA: Institute of Mental Measurements, Gryphon Press.

BUTCHER, H.J., AINSWORTH, M. and NESBITT, J.E. (1963) 'Personality factors and school achievement,' *British Journal of Educational Psychology*, 33, 276—85.

BUZZARD, R.B. (1971) 'Obituary to Sir Frederick Bartlett,' *Occupational Psychology*, 45, 1, 1—6.

CAMPBELL, D.T. and FISKE, D.W. (1959) 'Convergent and discriminant validation by the multitrait-multimethod matrix,' *Psychological Bulletin*, 56, 2.

CARROLL, J.B. (1974) 'Psychometric tests as cognitive tasks,' *ETS Research Bulletin*, (RB—74—16).

CATTELL, R.B. (1933) 'Temperament tests — I. Temperament,' *British Journal of Psychology*, 23.

CATTELL, R.B. (1943) 'The description of personality I: Foundations of trait measurement,' *Psychological Review*, 50, 6, 559—92.

CATTELL, R.B. (1943) 'The description of personality: Basic traits resolved into clusters,' *Journal of Abnormal and Social Psychology*, 38, 476—506.

CATTELL, R.B. (1944) 'Psychological measurement: Normative, ipsative, interactive,' *Psychological Review*, 51, 292—303.

CATTELL, R.B. (1944) 'Interpretation of the twelve primary personality factors,' *Character and Personality*, 13, 55—91.

CATTELL, R.B. (1946) *The Description and Measurement of Personality*. New York: World Book Company.

CATTELL, R.B. (1950) 'The main personality factors in questionnaire self-estimate material,' *Journal of Social Psychology* 31, 3—38.

CATTELL, R.B. (1956) 'Validation and intensification of the 16PF,' *Journal of Clinical Psychology*, 12, 205—14.

CATTELL, R.B. (1956) 'Second order personality factors in the questionnaire realm,' *Journal of Consulting Psychology*, 20, 6.

CATTELL, R.B. (1957) *Personality and Motivation Structure and Measurement*. New York: World Book Company.

CATTELL, R.B. (1962) 'The basis of recognition and interpretation of factors,' *Educational and Psychological Measurement*, XXII, 4.

CATTELL, R.B. (1964) 'Objective personality tests: a reply to Dr Eysenck,' *Occupational Psychology*, 38, 2.

CATTELL, R.B. (1965) *The Scientific Analysis of Personality*. London: Pelican Books.

CATTELL, R.B. (1966) 'The Scree test for the number of factors,' *Multivariate Behavioral Research*, 1, 245—76.

CATTELL, R.B. (1966) *Handbook of Multivariate Experimental Psychology*. Chicago: Rand McNally and Co.

CATTELL, R.B. (1968) 'Trait-view theory of perturbations in ratings and self-ratings (L (BR) — and Q Data): Its application to obtaining pure trait score estimates in questionnaires,' *Psychological Review*, 75, 2, 96—113.

CATTELL, R.B. (1972) 'The 16PF and basic personality structure,' *Journal of Behavioral Sciences*, 1(4), 169—87.

CATTELL, R.B. (1972) *Tabular supplement (of Norms) No 2 to the 16PF handbook (for 1969—1970 editions of Forms C+D)*. Champaign, Illinois: Institute for Personality and Ability Testing.

CATTELL, R.B. (1973) *Personality and Mood by Questionnaire*. San Francisco: Jossey-Bass.

CATTELL, R.B. (1974) 'How good is the modern questionnaire? General principles for evaluation,' *Journal of Personality Assessment*, 38, 2.

CATTELL, R.B. (1974) 'A large sample cross-check on 16PF,' *The Journal*, Fall, 179—95.

CATTELL, R.B., BALCAR, K., HORN, J.L. and NESSELROADE, J.R. (1969) 'Factor matching procedures: An improvement of the Index; with Tables,' *Educational and Psychological Measurement*, 29.

CATTELL, R.B. and BUTCHER, J. (1968) *The Prediction of Achievement and Creativity*. Indianapolis: Bobbs-Merrill.

CATTELL, R.B. and CATTELL, M.D.L. (1968) *High School Personality Questionnaire (HSPQ)*. 1968—69 Edition. Champaign, Illinois: Institute for Personality and Ability Testing.

CATTELL, R.B. and EBER, H.W. (1967—70) *Sixteen Personality Factor Questionnaire (16PF) Forms A & B (1967—68 Edition) and Forms C & D (1969—70 Edition)*. Champaign, Illinois: Institute for Personality and Ability Testing.

CATTELL, R.B., EBER, H.W. and DELHEES, K. (1968) 'A large sample cross validation of the personality trait structure of the 16PF with some clinical implications,' *Multivariate Behavioral Research*, Special Issue, 107—32.

CATTELL, R.B., EBER, H.W. and TATSUOKA, M. (1970) *Handbook for the Sixteen Personality Factor Questionnaire (16PF)*. Champaign, Illinois: Institute for Personality and Ability Testing.

CATTELL, R.B. and NICHOLS, K.F. (1972) '*An improved definition* from ten researchers of second order personality factors in Q-data (With cross-cultural checks),' *Journal of Social Psychology*, 86, 187—203.

CATTELL, R.B. and RADCLIFFE, J.A. (1962) 'Reliabilities and validation of simple and extended weighted and buffered unifactor scales,' *British Journal of Statistical Psychology*, XV, 2.

CATTELL, R.B. and SCHEIER, I.H. (1961) *The Meaning and Measurement of Neuroticism and Anxiety*. New York: Ronald Press.

CATTELL, R.B. and SCHEIER, I.H. (1963) *IPAT Anxiety Scale Questionnaire (IAS)*. Champaign, Illinois: Institute for Personality and Ability Testing.

CATTELL, R.B. and TSUTIOKA, B. (1964) 'The importance of factor-trueness and validity versus homogeneity and orthogonality in test scales,' *Educational and Psychological Measurement*, XXIV, 1.

CATTELL, R.B. and WARBURTON, F.W. (1961) 'A cross-cultural comparison of patterns of extraversion and anxiety,' *British Journal of Psychology*, 52, 1, 3—15.

CHILD, D. (1969) 'A comparative study of personality, intelligence and social class in a technological university,' *British Journal of Educational Psychology*, 39, 40—6.

COOLEY, W.W. and LOHNES, P.R. (1971) *Multivariate Data Analysis*. New York: Wiley.

CORTIS, G.A. (1968) 'Predicting student performance in colleges of education,' *British Journal of Educational Psychology*, 38, 2, 115—22

CRONBACH, L.J. (1970) *Essentials of Psychological Testing*. Third Edition (1970). New York: Harper & Row International.

DARLINGTON, R.B. (1968) 'Multiple regression in psychological research and practice,' *Psychological Bulletin*, 69, 3, 161—82.

DEYOUNG, G.E. (1972) 'Standards of decision regarding personality factors in questionnaires,' *Canadian Journal of Behavioral Psychology*.

DICKEN, C.F. (1959) 'Simulated patterns on the Edwards Personal Preference Schedule,' *Journal of Applied Psychology*, 43, 372—78.

EBEL, ROBERT L. (1972) 'Why is a longer test usually a more reliable test?' *Educational and Psychological Measurement*, 32, 249—53.

EDWARDS, A.L. and ABBOTT, R.D. (1973) 'Relationships between the EPI scales and the 16PF, CPI and EPPS scales,' *Educational & Psychological Measurement*, 33, 231—38.

ENTWISTLE, N.J. (1972) 'Students and their academic performance in different types of institution.' In: (Ed Butcher, H.J. and Rudd, E.) *Contemporary Problems in Higher Education*. London: McGraw-Hill.

ENTWISTLE, N.J. and CUNNINGHAM, S. (1968) 'Neuroticism and school attainment: A linear relationship,' *British Journal of Educational Psychology*, 38, 123—32.

ENTWISTLE, N.J. and ENTWISTLE, D. (1970) 'The relationships between personality, study methods and academic performance,' *British Journal of Educational Psychology*, 40, II.

EYSENCK, H.J. (1947) *Dimensions of Personality*. London: Routledge.

EYSENCK, H.J. (1954) *The Psychology of Politics*. London: Routledge & Kegan Paul.

EYSENCK, H.J. (1960) *The Structure of Human Personality*. 2nd Edition. London: Methuen & Co.

EYSENCK, H.J. (1972) 'Primaries or second order factors: A critical consideration of Cattell's 16PF battery,' *British Journal of Social and Clinical Psychology*, II, 265—69.

EYSENCK, H.J. and EYSENCK, S.B.G. (1964) *Eysenck Personality Inventory*. London: Hodder & Stoughton.

EYSENCK, H.J. and EYSENCK, S.B.G. (1969) *Personality Structure and Measurement*. London: Routledge & Kegan Paul.

EYSENCK, H.J. and EYSENCK, S.B.G. (1975) *Eysenck Personality Questionnaire*. London: Hodder & Stoughton.

EYSENCK, S.B.G. and EYSENCK, H.J. (1972) 'The questionnaire measurement of psychoticism,' *Psychological Medicine*, 2, 1, 50—55.

GOLDBERG, L.R. (1970) Why Measure that Trait? An Historical Analysis of Personality Scales and Inventories. Tutorial Address to Western Psychological Assoc., Los Angeles.

GROSS, A.L., FAGGEN, J. and MCCARTHY, K. (1974) 'The differential predictability of the college performance of males and females,' *Educational and Psychological Measurement*, 34, 363—65.

GUILFORD, J.P. (1954) *Psychometric Methods*. 2nd Edition. New York: McGraw Hill Book Co.

GUILFORD, J.P. (1959) *Personality*. New York: McGraw-Hill Book Co.

GUILFORD, J.P. and ZIMMERMAN, W.S. (1949—55) *The Guilford-Zimmerman Temperament Survey*. Orange, California: Sheridan Psychological Services Inc.

HARTMAN, B.J. (1966) 'Personality factors of the Cattell 16PF test and hypnotic susceptibility,' *Psychological Reports*, 19, 1337—1338.

HOLLAND, J.L. and ASTIN, A.W. (1962) 'The prediction of the academic, artistic, scientific and social achievement of undergraduates of superior scholastic aptitude,' *Journal of Educational Psychology*, 53, 3, 132—43.

HOWARTH, E. and BROWNE, J.A. (1971) 'An item factor analysis of the 16PF,' *Personality*, 2, 2.

HOWARTH, E. and BROWNE, J.A. (1972) 'An item factor analysis of the Eysenck Personality Inventory,' *British Journal of Social and Clinical Psychology*, 11, 162—74.

HOWARTH, E., BROWNE, J.A. and MARCEAU, R. (1972) 'An item analysis of Cattell's 16PF,' *Canadian Journal of Behavioral Sciences Review*, 4 (1).

HUDSON, L. (1972) *The Cult of the Fact*. London: Jonathan Cape.

JOHNSGARD, K.W. and OGILVIE, B.C. (1968) 'The competitive racing driver: A preliminary report,' *Journal of Sports Medicine and Physical Fitness*, 8, 87—95.

KARSON, S. and POOL, K.B. (1958) 'Second order factors in personality measurement,' *Journal of Consulting Psychology*, 22, 4.

KELVIN, P.R., LUCAS, C.V. and OJHA, A.B., (1965) 'The relationship between personality, mental health and academic performance in university students,' *British Journal of Social and Clinical Psychology*, 4, 244.

KLINE, P. (1966) 'Extraversion, neuroticism and performance among Ghanaian university students,' *British Journal of Educational Psychology*, 36, 92—94.

LEACH, P.J. (1967) 'A critical study of the literature concerning rigidity,' *British Journal of Social and Clinical Psychology*, 6, 11—22.

LEVONIAN, E. (1961) 'Personality measurement with items selected from the 16PF,' *Educational and Psychological Measurement*, XXI, 4.

LEVONIAN, E. (1961) 'Statistical analysis of the 16PF,' *Educational and Psychological Measurement*, XXI, 3.

LEVY, P. (1973) 'On the relation between test theory and psychology.' In: KLINE, P. (ed) *New Approaches in Psychological Measures*. London: Wiley.

LEWIS, J. (1974) 'Undergraduate ability-achievement and the earning of graduate degrees,' *Educational and Psychological Measurement*, 34, 383—85.

LORD, F.M. and NOVICK, M.R. (1968) *Statistical Theories of Mental Test Scores*. Menlo Park, California: Addison-Wesley Pub Co.

LYNN, R. (1959) 'Two personality characteristics related to academic achievement,' *British Journal of Educational Psychology*, 29, 213—16.

MEEHL, P. (1945) 'The dynamics of 'structured' personality tests,' *Journal of Clinical Psychology*, 1, 296—303.

MICHAELIS, W. and EYSENCK, H.J. (1971) 'The determination of personality inventory factor patterns and intercorrelations by changes in real-life motivation,' *Journal of Genetic Psychology*, 118, 223—34.

MORRIS, J. and MARTIN, J. (1972) *Computer Personnel Selection — 2: Programmers*. Manchester: National Computing Centre.

MURRAY, H.A. (1938) *Explorations in Personality*. London: Oxford University Press.

NAYLOR, F.D. (1972) *Personality and Educational Achievement*. Sydney: John Wiley & Sons Australasia Pty Ltd.

NIE, N., BENT, D. and HULL, C. (1970) *Statistical Package for the Social Sciences*. New York: McGraw-Hill.

NOWAKOWSKA, M. (1974) 'Polish adaptation of the 16PF as a source of cross-cultural comparisons,' *Polish Psychological Bulletin*, 5, 1.

NUNNALLY, J.C. (1967) *Psychometric Theory*. New York: McGraw-Hill.

OVERALL, J.G. and KLETT, C.J. (1972) *Applied Multivariate Analy-*

sis. New York: McGraw-Hill.

SAVAGE, R.D. (1972) 'Personality factors and academic performance,' In: NAYLOR, F.D. (Ed.) *Personality and Educational Achievement*. Sydney: John Wiley & Sons Australasia Pty Ltd.

SAVILLE, P. (1972) *The British Standardisation of the 16PF: Supplement of Norms, Forms A and B*. Windsor: NFER Publishing Co.

SAVILLE, P. (1973) 'The standardisation of an adult personality inventory on the British population,' *Bulletin of the British Psychological Society*, 26, 25—29.

SAVILLE, P. and BLINKHORN, S. (1976) *British Undergraduate Norms to the 16PF (Forms A and B)*. Windsor: NFER Publishing Co.

SAVILLE, P. and BLINKHORN, S. (1976) *British Undergraduate Norms to the 16PF (Forms C and D)*. Windsor: NFER Publishing Co.

SAVILLE, P. and BLINKHORN, S. (1976) *British Undergraduate Norms to the IPAT Anxiety Scale, Neuroticism Scale Questionnaire and the Eysenck Personality Inventory* (Form A). Windsor: NFER Publishing Co.

SAVILLE, P. and FINLAYSON, L. (1973) *British Supplement to the High School Personality Questionnaire (Form A) Anglicised 1968/69 Edition*. Windsor: NFER Publishing Co.

SCHAIE, K.W. (1962) 'On the equivalence of questionnaire and rating data,' *Psychological Reports*, 10, 521—22.

SCHEIER, I.H. and CATTELL, R.B. (1961) *Neuroticism Scale Questionnaire*. Champaign, Illinois: Institute for Personality and Ability Testing.

SEASHORE, H.G. (1962) 'Women are more predictable than men,' *Journal of Counselling Psychology*, 9, 3, 261—70.

SPIELBERGER, C.D., GORSUCH, R.L. and LUSHENE, R. (1970) *State-Trait Anxiety Inventory*. Palo Alto, California: Consulting Psychologists Press.

START, K.B. (1966) 'The relation of teaching ability to measures of personality,' *British Journal of Educational Psychology*, 36, 158—65.

START, K.B. (1968) 'Rater-ratee personality in the assessment of teaching ability,' *British Journal of Educational Psychology*, 38, 14—20.

SUHR, V.W. (1953) 'The Cattell 16PF as a prognosticator of accident susceptibility,' *Proceedings of the Iowa Academy of Science*, 60, 558—61.

TATSUOKA, M.M. (1972) *Selected Topics in Advanced Statistics*. Champaign, Illinois: Institute for Personality and Ability Testing.

TATSUOKA, M.M. and CATTELL, R.B. (1970) 'Linear equations for estimating a person's occupational adjustment based on information on occupational profiles,' *British Journal of Educational Psychology*, 40, 3.

TAYLOR, A.J.W. (1966) 'Beatlemania — A study in adolescent enthusiasm,' *British Journal of Social and Clinical Psychology*, 5, 81—88.

UNIVERSITY GRANTS COMMITTEE (UGC) (1975) *Statistics in Education: Universities Vol 6*. London: HMSO.

VAUGHAN, D. (1973) 'The relative methodological soundness of several major personality factor analyses,' *Journal of Behavioural Sciences*, 5.

VERNON, P.E. (1964) *Personality Assessment*. London: Methuen & Co.

WARBURTON, F.W., BUTCHER, H.J. and FORREST, G.M. (1963) 'Predicting student performance in a university department of education,' *British Journal of Educational Psychology*, 33, 68—79.

WISEMAN, S. (1973) 'The educational obstacle race — Factors which hinder pupil performance,' *Educational Research*, 15, 2, 87—93.

ZWEIG, F. (1964) *The Student in the Age of Anxiety*. New York: Free Press (MacMillan Co).